THE MISSING KENNEDY

ROSEMARY KENNEDY
AND THE SECRET BONDS OF FOUR WOMEN

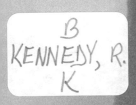
ELIZABETH KOEHLER-PENTACOFF

Published by Bancroft Press
"Books That Enlighten"
P.O. Box 65360
Baltimore, MD 21209
410.358.0658 *phone*
410.764.1967 *fax*

www.bancroftpress.com

ISBN
978-1-61088-174-6 hardcover

Author Photo Courtesy of Mahesh R. Junnarkar
Cover and Interior Design by J. L. Herchenroeder
Printed in the United States

For Sister Paulus and Rosie

Contents

ACKNOWLEDGMENTS

Writing a book is a communal effort. I'm particularly grateful to my writing friends, especially Beverly Lauderdale and Karen Terhune, who served as readers and offered essential feedback, support, and advice.

Without Ellen Leroe's encouragement and specific help on writing a query letter, I'd still be working on its first draft.

Susan Taylor Brown, Ginger Wadsworth, Abigail Samoun, Barbara Bentley, and Fran Wojnar also deserve my gratitude for their friendship and advice.

Every writer should be so fortunate in discovering researchers who know their material and share their expertise. Special recognition goes to Robert Murphy, President of the Beacon Historical Society, and Sandy Moneymaker of the Beacon Historical Society, for their information on Craig House; Supervisory Park Ranger Jim Roberts, Chief of Visitor Services, and Christine Wirth, Archivist Specialist, who answered my questions about the John Fitzgerald Kennedy National Historic Site; Kate McKenna, Editorial and Multimedia Director of Special Olympics; The librarians of The National Oceanographic Data's Central Library in Silver Spring, Maryland for their prompt responses about weather on particular days in historic Boston; Dr. Steven Holtz, neurologist on the faculty of University of California, Berkeley, for information about the human brain; Andrea Speth, Vice President of Marketing and Community Relations, Saint Coletta; Karen Gallagher and Mark Zastrow, Directors of Development, Saint Coletta, for history and facts about Saint Coletta; Jean L. Merry, Communications Director of the Sisters of Saint Francis of Assisi, and Sister Cecila Struck,

Congregation Archivist for the Sisters of Saint Francis of Assisi, for information on my aunt's vows; and most of all, the staff at the John F. Kennedy Presidential Library, especially Reference Archivist Steve Plotkin, Audio Visual Archivist Emily Watlington, and Intellectual Property Manager Lee Statham.

I am deeply appreciative of the helpful interviews and support from Anthony Shriver, Bobby Shriver, and Mark Shriver.

Thank you to my cousins whose memories enriched the book and reinforced my own recollections: Mary Koehler, Ellen Sauer, Bob and Pat Sterle, Joanne Riordan, Patricia Bacon, Arlene Condon, Mary Konop, Marge Wenzel, and my father's cousins, Marion Igl and Ann Tabot.

I am lucky to have had the help of Arnold Koehler's written memories. My father's brother, he served as the family's unofficial historian.

I am likewise fortunate to have had the written memories of my father and especially of Sister Paulus.

Little did I know that when my husband videotaped my interviews of Sister Paulus, my father, and his siblings about their youth, one day these conversations would be useful for a book. The original purpose of the interviews was a desire to know more about our family.

I must express gratitude to the Sisters of Saint Francis of Assisi who served at Saint Coletta: I have been honored to have grown up surrounded by their loving presence.

By their actions, my parents showed me what kindness really is. They were a perfectly suited pair to raise someone like me: opinionated and yet spiritual. I only wish I would have written this book sooner, so I could have talked with my parents again about incidents I was too young to remember.

Because I am anything but computer-savvy, I'm fortunate in having a son who is. I'm also lucky he comes up with instant, common sense solutions. Thank you, Tofer. I have a feeling the older I get, the more I will be relying on you for more than computer knowledge.

Thank you to my editor and designer at Bancroft Press, and to the publisher.

Finally, my utmost thanks and love to my husband, Bob, not just for his assistance in helping me conduct research at the JFK Presidential Library, and his continual support during the writing of this book, but for our lives together.

INTRODUCTORY NOTE

Although *intellectually disabled* is the preferred term today for impaired cognitive function, *mentally retarded* was a common label used throughout the twentieth century. It is used, when applicable to the time period, within this book.

Rosemary's Childhood

At Rose and Joe Kennedy's Beals Street home, the cloud-covered skies showed no signs of clearing as rain sprinkled down against the upstairs bedroom window. Rose lay in her bed feeling a concern she couldn't quite place. During neither of her pregnancies had she carried any sense of foreboding, and she had given birth to two bright, healthy, energetic sons, Joe Jr. and Jack.

Perhaps her apprehension was partly due to the uneasiness prevailing in the country. At President Wilson's request, the U.S. Congress had declared war against Germany the year before, and in both its morning and evening editions, the *Boston Globe* newspapers were reporting on the latest hostilities. Because of those stories, Rose was well aware that German spies could be lurking anywhere. They could even be spying on her husband Joe at Bethlehem Steel. Joe managed the company's shipping operation, which was heavily supplying the Allies with manufacturing materiel for their munitions.

Then there was a worry closer to home and far more insidious—the strange and deadly flu then assaulting the nation. Who could not help but be under its dark spell? The Spanish influenza had begun only a few miles away, right in Boston. Within two weeks of its outbreak, more than two thousand people had been afflicted, with pregnant women and young people especially predisposed to the illness. Before the epidemic was over, it would kill 105 million people world-wide and take the lives of 650,000 in the United States, with 45,000 of those deaths recorded in Massachusetts alone.

Where is Dr. Good? the twenty-eight-year-old Rose wondered. *He should be here by now. The baby is coming.*

The nurse grabbed Rose's knees and forced them together, telling her not to push and to wait for the doctor. Raised in the Victorian era and well-educated by strict Catholic nuns, Rose had learned to do what she was told. She would not disobey a physician, or even a nurse filling in for one. Rose followed the nurse's instructions and did not push.

When Rose Marie (known as Rosemary, and nicknamed Rosie) Kennedy was born on September 13, 1918, her mother noticed almost right away that she was different. In the weeks following her first daughter's birth, the infant rarely cried. Unlike her boisterous and lively older brothers, little Rosemary was mostly quiet. Had Dr. Good's delayed arrival deprived the newborn of oxygen at a critical time? There is no way to know authoritatively.

In *Times to Remember*, her memoir, Rose Fitzgerald Kennedy wrote of Rosemary, "She was slow in everything, and some things she seemed unable to learn how to do, or do well or with consistency. When she was old enough for childish sports, I noticed, for instance, that she couldn't steer her sled. When she was old enough to learn a little reading and writing, the letters and words were extremely difficult for her, and instead of writing from left to right on a page, she wrote in the opposite direction." [1]

In a letter to Santa requesting several Christmas presents, which Rosemary probably wrote when she was between eight and ten years old, it's clear she didn't understand punctuation or sentence structure, had memorized various spelling words that didn't make sense within the context of her request, and had misspelled about one out of every five words.

Trusting her instincts, Rose was skeptical of the doctors' I.Q. tests, even though she would later claim she was never told of Rosemary's specific results. In the 1920s, few questioned how various learning disabilities and testing techniques affected a person's intelligence.

After Rosemary's birth, Rose and Joe's family grew rapidly. Within the space of twelve years, six more children were added to their brood. Mrs. Kennedy would sometimes watch Kathleen, born less than two years after Rosemary, playing with her numerous friends. She didn't have to worry about little "Kick" being slow or inactive, or not fitting in with others.

Three happy Kennedy children: Rosie, Jack, and Joe

*Five gorgeous Kennedy kids: Rosie with her two older brothers,
and her younger sisters Kathleen and Eunice (taken circa 1923)*

For two years of kindergarten, Rosemary was sent to a local
public school, Edward Devotion, on Harvard Street in Brookline.
But when she didn't show herself to be proficient in the appropriate
ways, administrators tested her. They discovered Rosemary to be
deficient in basic cognitive skills expected of someone her age. She
also didn't interact well with her fellow students. But the school had
a problem: It couldn't hold Rosie back and put her through a third
year of kindergarten.

Rosemary did not return to Edward Devotion in September
1925. Wanting the best possible medical attention for their daughter,
Rose and Joe sought out the head of the Psychology Department at
Harvard University. After tests were conducted, doctors informed
them Rosemary was mentally retarded.

In a 1975 magazine article, Rose Kennedy recalled how she responded upon hearing the diagnosis: ". . . My first reaction was shock and surprise. Like all mothers, I had prayed that my child would be born normal and healthy . . . I had to endure the anguish of every mother who learns that her child will have to face the world with a devastating handicap."[2]

Rosie enjoys a three-wheeler by the sea

Rose and Joe were desperate to learn how to help their handicapped daughter. What could they do? Harvard doctors advised them to institutionalize Rosemary, indicating that doing so was best for all involved.

Put her away? Rose and Joe wouldn't consider the possibility, even for the shortest time.

"[The situation] was nerve wracking, incomprehensible, and for my husband and me, unprecedented," recalled Mrs. Kennedy. [3]

Joe and Rose agreed they could never let Rosemary live in an institution for the mentally retarded. Their daughter would be miserable, lonely, and physically at risk.

Together, Rose and Joe Kennedy fought for a more desirable life for Rosemary, enlisting their whole family in the effort. The parents gathered together older sons Joe Jr. and Jack and explained that Rosemary was "a little slow," so she'd need love and help from both of them. They came to realize Rosemary thrived on extra patience and kindness. Neither of them played practical jokes on Rosie, as they did on one another and on their other siblings, because they knew it would be cruel. Because she couldn't and wouldn't understand their humor, Rosemary would feel mistreated.

The boys understood: They were Kennedys, and the family stuck together.

Later, as the other Kennedy children grew up and recognized Rosie's disabilities on their own, they learned from Jack and Joe Jr., and their parents how to treat her.

In *True Compass: A Memoir*, Ted Kennedy wrote about how his older brother Jack would deal with Rosemary: "I recalled the gentle, natural ways in which he would look after Rosemary—always including her in the sailing expeditions with the rest of us. Compassion was the center of his soul . . . but he never wore it on his sleeve." [4]

Rosemary's First Communion, 1926

From the time she was eight until the age of sixteen, Rosie remained at home and worked with the best tutors and specialists the Kennedys could find. Her mother dedicated long hours to sit by her side and work with her too.

When the infant child of pilot Charles Lindbergh was kidnapped for ransom in 1932 and later found dead, Rose and Joe's fears for Rosemary grew. They decided Rosie must never be allowed to venture out alone.

In 1934, at the age of sixteen, Rosemary was accepted into Elmhurst Sacred Heart Convent, and Joe and Rose were ecstatic. Their daughter would be educated by nuns and learn how to relate to other young women, something they believed she sorely needed.

As it turned out, Rosemary lived at Elmhurst Sacred Heart Convent for just two years until she plateaued at the fourth grade level. She then returned home, where she was once again tutored by specialists and her mother.

Rose printed out letters for Rosie to copy. And she read to her. Rosie worked on her arithmetic, and Rose played tennis and catch with her daughter in hopes of improving Rosie's coordination. Rosemary correctly added together three triple-digit numbers, but had great difficulty reading, printing, and writing. Rose rewarded her daughter with smiles and quick praise whenever she succeeded. Rosie's eyes would glow.

As a teenager, Rosemary wanted to be treated the same as her siblings. She asked her mother why *she* couldn't go anywhere by herself. After all, her younger sisters were allowed to.

Rose tried to explain how sweet and innocent she was, and how her safety was at stake. She prayed her daughter would understand. She continued to worry about Rosemary's naïveté.

But Rosie detested the constant supervision and the unequal treatment. She decided to *prove* to her family that she could manage on her own. When no one was looking, Rosie would sneak away. Once beyond the view of those at home, she barreled across the yard and down the street.

More often than not, after Rosemary's escape attempts were thwarted, her frustrations boiled over—she erupted into an uncontrollable tantrum. Screaming like a wild animal, she would fall to the ground, her arms and legs flailing as she kicked and cried out in rage.

Her family was astounded. *Why was sweet, gentle Rosie acting this way?*

There was no way for them to know Rosie's situation had been incorrectly diagnosed. Her emotional responses aggravated a complicated underlying condition: mental illness.

Rosie as a freckle-faced fifteen-year-old

MY AUNT STELLA

Stella Koehler woke at dawn on her southeastern Wisconsin farm. Kneeling beside her bed, she whispered, "Dear God, please let there be a mink in the traps today. And bless Mother and Dad, Lucille, Leo, Arnold and Albert—" she took a breath before naming her five other brothers and sisters—"Anita, Paul, Florence, little Carl, and baby Elmer."

"You coming, Stella?" her older brother Arnold called from the hallway.

"Yes, I'll be right there," she said, as she flipped over her wall calendar from August to September 1920. Five days after Christmas that year, she'd turn eleven years old.

Before heading outside, Stella neatly folded her sheets and blankets over her bed. Her sisters did the same with theirs in the bedroom they shared downstairs. Peering from her window, she saw the breeze blowing the trees outside. Grabbing her jacket, she met Arnold and Leo in the parlor.

"Ready!" she said. As they did almost every day, they'd check the animal traps before breakfast.

Stella's heart pounded as they hiked from their backyard

vegetable garden down to the long grass of the marshy creek, which sparkled with dew. Though small and slender, Stella nearly kept up with her lanky brothers' long strides. *What will we find in our traps today?* All the Koehlers pitched in to keep their sixty-acre farm afloat during the lean years of the 1920s and '30s.

Muskrat will fetch only two or three dollars, but a mink could earn fifteen! And what will we do with any money earned?

Those new Baby Ruth chocolate bars Stella and her siblings so loved cost a nickel. *No, we won't waste our hard-earned cash on candy. Instead, we'll save for gifts for Mother and Dad.*

Each of the Koehler siblings went to a different area at the creek's edge to survey their own traps. Stella's long skirt dampened as she knelt to check hers. Dark brown fur extended from the metal contraption. "Muskrat!" she called. Any trapped critter was better than an empty trap.

"Muskrat here too!" yelled Arnold.

"Mink!" cried Leo.

The three jumped up and down and shouted at Leo's good news.

"By golly, you did it!" said Arnold, patting Leo on the back.

As she began to empty her trap, a wet nose poked Stella in her face. "Bowser!" She laughed. The family's black and white shepherd was wagging his tail.

The three raced Bowser back to the house and washed up in the shanty.

At the breakfast table, Stella put baby Elmer on her lap and fed him. As he giggled and cooed, she spooned him mashed bananas and oatmeal. "After I pick strawberries, I'll take you for a buggy ride," she promised him.

"The Tabats need us to pick their strawberries," said Anita.

"Good," said Stella. "That's two cents a box!"

"Today is our day for cleaning church," said Mother. "So

strawberry picking will have to wait."

As Stella washed the breakfast dishes with Anita, she saw Mother picking dahlias, mums, and morning glories for the church altar.

Stella and Mother sat on the buckboard while Nellie the horse pulled their carriage the mile and a half to Saint Bruno's Church in Dousman. The wagon wheels bumped along on graveled Highway Z, and as they passed by, the two waved at the Gramling and Bischel boys working in their fields. Nellie then turned in at the yellow-brick church, its steeple rising tall above the trees and surrounding cemetery.

Saint Bruno's sat behind a wrought-iron fence. The bell in the turret announced church services, funerals, weddings, and other celebrations in their small community. As Stella and Kathryn entered the chapel, they dipped their fingers into the holy water in the vessel by the door and genuflected.

Saint Bruno's Church

Inside, Stella began to dust and polish the brass candlesticks until they glimmered in the morning light. Next, she arranged their flowers in large vases. Kathryn complimented her daughter on her artistic arrangement as she shook out the clean linens she had brought with her and placed them on the altar. Before they left, they knelt in a pew and prayed together, crossing themselves as they rose to leave.

Stella (right) at her First Communion

When they arrived home, Anita ran out to meet them. "Stella! Stella!" she cried. "A baby chick died."

"Stella," said Mother. "Go ahead and have your funeral. You can pick strawberries after lunch."

Anita showed Stella the chick, which she had tucked into a matchbox in preparation for burial. Stella picked turnips from the garden and washed them under the pump, then sliced them thin to resemble Holy Communion wafers.

At the ensuing funeral, seven-year-old Paul served as priest, foreshadowing the role that would become his life's work. He stood in silence in the grape arbor while the children sat on wooden benches.

"Let's begin with 'Amazing Grace,'" said Paul.

Their clear voices echoed through the arbor and onto the farm fields, where Father, his two brothers, and a teenage neighbor boy cut clover seed. Stella settled Elmer in the buggy. His wide blue eyes watched the sun stream through the leaves, casting delicate patterns on the ground. The air smelled like walnuts, damp earth, and the knotty pine boards on which they sat. Carl stood at Stella's side, holding onto her skirt.

Paul read from his missal. "Let us pray for this baby chick," he said, "and let God repent the chick's sins and ours, so that he may be lifted into the Holy Spirit and be blessed unto heaven."

The children lined up to receive "Communion," with Arnold serving as the altar boy. As Stella knelt on the leaves and dirt, she prayed for the chick that was now in heaven. *Did baby chicks have sins?* she wondered. If not, at least the children's mass might help it get close to God.

Paul looked up to the sky, declaring as he raised his hands heavenward: "Eternal rest grant unto the faithful departed, oh Lord."

"And let the perpetual light shine upon them," his brothers and sisters responded together.

"May they rest in peace," said their priest.

"Amen," said everyone.

They filed out singing, "Holy God, We Praise Thy Name."

Not long after the chick's funeral, Baby Elmer woke to a burning fever and a cough so severe he could barely breathe.

Stella's mother was distraught. No medicines could be relied upon to cure such a serious illness. She placed her hat firmly on her head. "Dad, Uncle Charlie, and I are going to Holy Hill," referring to the Roman Catholic shrine twenty miles away. Turning to Lucille, the oldest child, she instructed her to keep a vigil with Elmer. Lucille nodded.

Stella and her brothers and sisters knelt and prayed. As Elmer's fever raged, his little face scrunched up every time he coughed, and he wheezed with every breath he took. But after a time, they noticed a change, and soon enough, Elmer drifted off to sleep.

When the Chevy pulled back into the driveway, Stella ran out of the house, the screen door slamming behind her. She jumped on the running board and leaned into the window. "Elmer's better! He isn't coughing!"

❀❖❀

For their bird club, Stella's brothers had built a clubhouse attached to the grape arbor, and everyone gathered there once a week for a meeting.

Leo called out the children's names for roll.

"Elmer?"

"Aye," answered Stella for him, as he sat in the pram next to her. She didn't want him to feel left out. Stella felt an especially close bond to her youngest sibling. Even as a ten-year-old, she was highly sensitive to the feelings of others, and especially those unable to take care of themselves.

But Stella was also spirited, and she craved a bit of excitement. After the bird club adjourned that afternoon, she pushed Elmer in the large baby buggy Al had remade from a smaller 1860s pram.

"Let's go for a quick walk, Elmer," she said.

A car whizzed by and the breeze ruffled her hair, lifting it from her neck, which had grown hot and sweaty from the summer sun. *How fast can I go?* Her shoes slapped against the dirt road, and the buggy's wheels kicked up clouds of dust. But she ran so swiftly, her hands slipped from the handle and the carriage and Elmer sailed ahead, bumping along on the dirt road until . . . *Crash!*

The runaway buggy hit a tree.

Stella gasped. "Elmer!" she cried.

She raced to the buggy, breathless, and peered inside. There was Elmer, his large blue eyes wide with surprise, and his round little mouth open, as if to say, "What happened? That was fun. Let's do it again!"

Elmer Koehler kneels beside his daughter (the author),
as a baby, in the family buggy

After Stella graduated from the eighth grade, she stayed home to help her mother run the household. But even then she longed to do something more. *What will I do with my life?* she thought. Her question wasn't answered until Stella reached her twenties.

The phone rang—two long rings and a single short one, which signaled that the call was for Stella's family, not to one of the fifteen other parties that shared the line. On the Koehlers' calls, those other parties often listened in, extracting bits of gossip that spread throughout the Scuppernogg area.

Stella picked up the receiver. "Hello, may I speak to Stella?" said the caller. She instantly recognized the serious-sounding voice as that of Saint Bruno's parish priest.

"Hello, Father!" she said.

"This summer, will you pick up the Sisters of St. Francis of Assisi nuns from Saint Coletta in the morning and bring them out here to teach vacation school?" he asked. "They'll need a ride home too, and on Saturday, they'll have to go to Holy Hill. Can you handle this, my dear?"

"I love driving, Father. I'd be honored to do this for the nuns," she said.

As it turned out, Stella's talks with the sisters during those summer drives helped her discover her true calling.

"One day I woke up and just knew I was happiest serving God. It was like a light bulb went off in my soul," she recalled many years later. But realizing her calling and acting on it were two separate matters.

Despite her resolution to serve God, Stella knew her mother needed her on the farm. How would she break the news that she intended to leave? Kathryn had already relinquished one of her boys, Paul, to the church seminary. Having a son become a priest was the highest accomplishment of a Catholic family.

DEC • 62

Holy Hill

But a girl? A nun carried less power within the church. And Stella did the work of several people at home. Although sister Anita lived there too, her health was very frail. How would her mother manage without her?

Stella didn't know how to tell her mother she planned to devote her life to God, but her calling pulled at her. The days and weeks blended one into another. When her three brothers—they still lived at home—came in from the fields, she helped her mother get the food on the table and clean up afterwards, just in time to begin the next meal. The list of other chores—cleaning, doing laundry, sewing and mending, gardening, caring for the chickens, collecting and selling their eggs, and tending the strawberry patch—was practically endless. And Stella devoted many hours each week to helping at

Saint Bruno's. She and her mother could barely handle all the work now. How could Mother do it without Stella?

Finally, Stella could wait no longer. One night after the supper dishes were put away, she and Mother sat down to work on the mending.

Stella stopped her sewing and looked right at her mother, the kerosene lamp illuminating Stella's blue eyes. "I've decided what I need to do with my life."

"Mmm," said Kathryn. "What would that be?"

"I want to go to the convent."

Kathryn stopped threading the needle and met her daughter's gaze. Stella could tell by the look on her face that the news was a surprise.

The old clock in the parlor bonged seven times before her mother spoke. "I need to think," she said.

Stella nodded. *At least she didn't say no.*

That night, after everyone else was asleep, Kathryn paced in the kitchen. She put her hand on the old pump and stared at the wood stove. *Who would collect wood? Help with the washing? Weed the vegetable garden?* She patted the gray hair in her bun. She wasn't getting any younger. But she knew that eventually she'd figure out a solution. She just needed time.

Meanwhile, in the girls' bedroom, Stella knelt by her bedside, praying the rosary in hopes her mother would allow her to become a nun.

The next morning, when Stella brought the chicken eggs into the house, her mother nodded toward her.

Stella set the egg basket on the table, sat down, and waited. Her mother wiped her hands on her flour sack apron. "You can go to the convent on one condition." She paused, gazing out the window at the chicken house, her brow furrowed.

Stella was frozen in place, her hand still on the egg basket's handle. "What's the condition?"

"Wait one year," said her mother.

Stella's heavy heart lightened. *She hadn't said no!* Although a year seemed like a long time, she knew she could get through it with God's help. She would cross the days off on the calendar and give up the year ahead for the Lord Jesus and for her mother, who desperately needed her on the farm.

"Thank you, Mother," she said, rising to hug her.

For a moment, they remained still, joined in a warm embrace. As they drew apart from each other, Stella saw the tears in her mother's eyes, and the weary slump of her shoulders.

In announcing the one-year condition to Stella's plan, Kathryn wasn't thinking only of her own workload. She understood that becoming a nun was a lifetime commitment. Testing her daughter's resolve was wise.

The Koehler family together, 1923

First Homes

As an adult, I visited Rosie's first home at 83 Beals Street in Brookline, Massachusetts, to get a sense of her early life and that of her famous family. The compact Victorian residence stands three stories tall on a small lot in the Boston suburb. It was easy to picture the young Kennedy children playing in the back yard.

Rose Kennedy wrote in *Times to Remember*, her 1974 autobiography: "It was a nice old wooden-frame house with clapboard siding; seven rooms, plus two small ones in the converted attic, all on a small lot with a few bushes and trees . . . about twenty-five minutes from the center of the city by trolley."[5]

The family home on Beals Street is now the John Fitzgerald Kennedy National Historic Site, run by the National Park Service. From the deep browns and reds of the rugs on the hardwood floors to the homey couch and chairs, the home felt warm and comfortable to me. I suppressed a desire to kick off my sandals and flop on the sofa.

The Kennedys' house on Beals Street, Rosie's first home

But my perspective as a child would have triggered a different impression. I would have whispered to my mother, "They're *rich!*" (I've since discovered that money isn't the only measure of wealth. There's wealth in memories, too.)

A lovely grand piano occupies one corner of the Kennedys' old living room. It was a wedding gift to Rose Kennedy from her uncles, and she delighted in playing her favorite song, "Sweet Adeline," on it. Although her children took piano lessons, Mrs. Kennedy lamented that her own passion never ignited a similar spark in any of her daughters. She did often ask Rosemary to perform, however.

I see an image of Rosemary declaring she couldn't, her hands stretching awkwardly across the keys. But her mother encouraged Rosie to practice, confident she'd improve. Rosemary plunked at the keys. But no matter how hard she tried, she couldn't make her hands obey her mind.

Mrs. Kennedy shook her head to soothe Rosie and to remind her to simply try her best. That was what she asked of all her children.

This image of Rosemary struggling to play the piano slipped away from me as the National Park Service tour guide led the group I was with to the bedrooms on the second floor.

"The third floor is now our office," the guide said.

"What was the third floor for originally?" I asked.

"The maids' rooms," she replied.

A relatively modest house, and yet young Rose and Joe Kennedy had live-in help? How different the Kennedys' family life must have been from the Koehlers' in the rolling hills of Wisconsin.

✺❂✺

In the Koehler farmhouse, the girls slept on the main floor and the boys slept in one large second-floor bedroom. Each child engraved his or her initials on a separate piece of wood placed in the oven on cold winter evenings. Before bedtime, the warm wood was removed from the oven and buried under the sheets on each bed, near the children's feet. In a home without central heating, staying warm required resourcefulness and creativity. My father and his brothers awoke to discover snow inside their bedroom window ledges; ice formed around their noses as they snuggled in their beds.

The Koehler farmhouse

✄◉✄

The Kennedy birthplace still stands with its original bassinet, a christening outfit and toys artfully scattered around.

The backdrop for the Koehler family was vastly different. I can imagine the farm children playing with handmade dolls or sticks. For them, a toy doll for the girls, and a truck for the boys were rarities. Even the Koehler baby buggy had been fashioned from a wooden Civil War-era pram, enlarged by older brother Al for the growing family.

Rosemary's childhood bedroom

The Koehler homestead, then unoccupied, burned down on September 11, 1970, set on fire by vandals who had broken in. Although it was by no means an historic event, I distinctly remember hearing about the farmhouse fire. My dad's cousin, Marion, phoned to tell me the news, and I let out a cry.

"It's all right," Marion said. "No one was hurt."

But it wasn't all right. The farmhouse had been my first home, and though I could no longer recall it, I knew, through fond stories my parents had told me, about our family life there.

For example, as a toddler, I joined my mother in the strawberry patch to "help" her pull weeds.

"Uh, uh, uh!" I announced, giggling with glee as I extended one hand over a plant, instead of a weed, and teasing my mother.

"No, no, no!" she shrieked with pretend horror, then sighing deeply with relief when I removed my hand from the plant.

Minutes later, I began the same game all over again.

Another beloved story recalled how my mother's whole family motored from Milwaukee to the farm because they loved its homey feeling and the pastoral setting—deer roaming the countryside and Dad's cows mooing contentedly in the pasture.

"We had so many good family times there," said my mother. "My family loved the farm."

So did I.

The farm had been the Koehler home since the turn of the twentieth century. It was not only my first home, but also the home of the grandparents I never met. The farm rooted me and my family in history; its deep roots were also the roots of our family tree.

As it turned out, the fire not only destroyed the farm but also dashed a dream of mine. The farm might not be on the national registry of historic places, but I longed to see where I had slept as a baby and to see where my Aunt Stella had rocked my dad next to the coal stove. Where had she shucked corn while Grandma baked biscuits? Where had Leo lain in agony, dying from an infected appendix? Where had Grandma Katie given birth to Dad, Stella, and eight other babies?

My mother, father, and I planted a grove of pine trees just beyond a bend curving away from the farmhouse. Those trees still stand today, a majestic testament to green living at a time when a young farm couple believed in the simple goodness and beauty of trees.

The Koehler family farmstead after the devastating fire

※❖※

In rural Wisconsin, my mother was known as a "city" girl, having lived in both Los Angeles and Milwaukee in her late teens and early twenties. So in 1949, at the age of twenty-nine, when she married my thirty-year-old father, farm life was as much a shock to her as city life was to the Koehlers and the staid farming community.

The author's mother before marriage

I have just a few treasured photos of my mother before and after she married. In the first she's done-up like a fashion model, mink coat and all. There's a glamour and confidence to her eyes and smile.

In another photo taken a few months later, after she and my father married, she's standing proudly, holding a basketful of eggs she'd just gathered from the chicken coop. She's wearing rolled-up overalls and an old jacket, a man's shirt tail hanging out in front. The large babushka covering her head billows in the wind. She stands next to a handmade sign—FOR SALE: EGGS. A bare tree stands alone in the stark landscape behind her.

The author's mother as a married woman in Wisconsin

When I saw those photos as I child, I wondered about my mother's sanity in choosing my father and their new rural existence. As a single woman, it appeared she had everything: good looks, glamour, and an exciting city life. The mink coat obviously indicated a past time of luxury.

But when I heard the story behind the photo, I realized that some important details can't be captured on film. Although Mom loved her job as a bookkeeper, her male bosses paid her much less than her male counterparts for the same work. When she quit her job to get married, they had to hire several men to replace her.

And the mink coat in the photo? She had borrowed it.

Some of my mother's happiest times were spent on the farm, gathering eggs from the persnickety chickens, kneading bread dough and setting it on the porch to rise, and feeling the fresh, moist earth between her fingers as she planted tomatoes in her vegetable garden.

But not all the memories were rosy. Earning enough money on a small farm wasn't easy. Fighting the elements was a struggle, and it was difficult to fit in among people who had known each other their entire lives and who had lived a certain unchanging way for generations. My mother recalled the time one local female eyed her and spit out these highly critical words: "Mother Mary never wore jeans."

When my father chose to sell the farm in 1959 and move to a small nearby town to work in a factory, Mom believed others blamed her for the move.

"City girl tells country boy what to do," she said.

"I didn't want to leave." She had loved the farm. "But we couldn't make a living at it," she said regretfully, as if admitting her own personal failure.

Although they liked their new house in town with its modern conveniences, and Dad enjoyed the security of a steady paycheck, my parents missed their first home and always would. They understood how I felt too. While growing up, I begged Dad to drive by the homestead farmhouse just so I could see it. I wished we had never moved. Had we stayed, animals and nature would have been part of my daily life.

Raising her eyebrows, my mother reminded me farm life had its drawbacks. "You wouldn't be able to go to the library," she said. "And you wouldn't have drama club after school. Your dad never got to be in the school band because he had to take the bus home and do his farm chores. And what about your friends visiting if you were way out in the country?" Mom shook her head.

She was right, of course. Getting up at 4:00 a.m. to milk cows or feed the chickens wouldn't be my idea of the way to start the day. But for years I imagined the horse I would have ridden or even owned.

What fantasies did Rosemary have? Did she have a sense of her family's history? Dream of sailing a boat alone on the Cape? Imagine a party with girlfriends instead of just her family members? Believe she would marry and share a home with a husband and children?

I imagine Rosie as a girl, wiggling her toes in the rough sand as seagulls squawk overhead.

Her younger sister, Eunice, challenges everyone to a race and the sisters fly along the shore, kicking up sand. Rosie laughs, the salty spray from the ocean waves sprinkling her face. She feels fresh and alive.

Eunice raises her hands high above her head and jumps up and down as she declares herself the winner. Rosie comes up from behind and claims Eunice got a head start.

Their good-natured teasing and sisterly banter continue as they laugh and run to their pool. While Eunice swims laps, Rosie floats on her back and listens to the smack of tennis balls on the family court, the cheers from a touch football game on the front lawn, and the clink of glasses from the porch.

The family's flag flaps in the breeze against the blue sky; lazy clouds float by. Eunice and Rosie dry off and go inside. Their mother is playing "When Irish Eyes are Smiling" and "Sweet Adeline" on the piano.

Rosie twirls around the overstuffed chairs and couches, pretending she's dancing. Home is her favorite place in the world. She never wants to leave, until she has her own home, of course.

After our farmhouse burned down, Dad took a picture of it and saved a few bricks. He mentioned the keepsakes to his family, but nobody at the time wanted one as a memento.

After my mother passed away in 2002, my father and I cleaned out the basement in my parents' home. We found the farmhouse bricks, priceless treasures that unleashed a flood of memories.

The night before I left Wisconsin for the trip home to California, my cousins held the Koehler family Friday night fish fry—a tradition for many families in Wisconsin, Catholic or not. By that time, Dad was the only one of ten siblings who was still alive. My cousins and I gathered in a large room at a local restaurant, with Dad as the honored patriarch.

"Don't go home yet," I said as my cousins began heading for their cars in the restaurant's parking lot.

"Why not?" asked my cousin Mary.

"We have something for everyone. Come with us," I said.

Dad and I popped the trunk, revealing the few bricks from the old farmhouse.

"These are the bricks I saved when the farmhouse burned," said Dad.

"You saved them?" asked my cousin Joanne, impressed.

Dad nodded.

"Do you want some pieces to take with you?" I asked.

"Yes!" my cousins replied in a chorus. Thirty of them clamored around the car, using my father's Colonial pocketknife from his childhood to chip away at the bricks so they could take home a piece of the Koehler Homestead Farm. We all basked in the excitement of that evening, a doorway to a continued connection among my Koehler cousins and me. Reconnecting with my extended family as an adult and recalling our shared history was a gift.

Blessed in other ways, Rosie may never have savored a similar perspective. In 1941, when she was twenty-three, she underwent a new procedure, a prefrontal lobotomy, intended to ease her emotional outbursts. It left her mentally and physically incapacitated the rest of her life.

When a homestead burns, a physical place is gone forever, but the remembrances remain in those who survive. Rosemary's lobotomy was like a fire; ashes of sorts flew up in its wake.

In the 63 years after her lobotomy, what remained behind Rosie's once bright, glowing eyes? Did she remember Beals Street? Or Hyannis Port?

ENGLAND

In 1938, when Rosie was nineteen years old, President Franklin Roosevelt appointed her father to be the United States Ambassador to England. The family's lives took a radical turn. It launched everyone from local Boston society to international attention.

After being led to elegant rooms as guests in King George and Queen Elizabeth's castle, Joe remarked to his wife, "Rose, this is a helluva long way from East Boston." [6]

Rose reminded Joe all about the haughty women who had refused to invite her to join Boston's Junior League and the Vincent Club. Joe remembered the stings all too well, too, including being denied membership to the Boston Country Club. They enjoyed a laugh together.

Rampant Irish prejudice didn't diminish much for certain Boston residents even in the early 1960s. While in the White House, Jack remarked, "Do you know it is impossible for an Irish Catholic to get into the Somerset Club in Boston? If I moved back to Boston even after being President, it would make no difference." [7]

Rose and Joe had endured Irish discrimination throughout their lives—plagued by the stereotype of the loud, drinking Irish laborer. They fought it with aristocratic behavior and wealth. As a result of Joe's perceptive financial investments and hard work, he had become a millionaire at thirty. Less than twenty years later, he was his country's chief emissary to its most important ally.

When Rosemary and Eunice arrived at No. 14 Prince's Gate, the palatial estate where the Kennedys resided, they wandered the castle wide-eyed at their new life of luxury. Everything was so fancy—it looked like they would be living in a museum!

When Rose Kennedy casually mentioned to Joe's friend William Randolph Hearst that many of the walls in their new home were bare, he loaned them paintings. Ancient tapestry adorned other walls. Chandeliers hung from high ceilings. Delicate Louis XIV furniture filled the ballroom. The curved marble staircase that led from the entrance hall was regal enough to welcome royalty but also great fun for children. Teddy, Bobby, Patricia, and Jean flew down the railing. *Whoosh!*

In 1938, a writer from *Vogue* described the Kennedys' English home as a "sober eighteenth-century family mansion." The amenities included "their own talkie machine installed at the Embassy." [8] Looking back on it today, it's hard to imagine that these words describe a *radio*.

"The American Ambassador and his family have swept like a conquering horde upon London, which has lowered its defenses and admitted itself stormed . . . There can have been few ambassadorial appointments which caused more brouhaha than this . . ." [9] Headlines waxed hysteric on both sides of the Atlantic: English newspapers caught something of America's overtones, and it seemed as if the Kennedys often appeared in bigger, blacker type than any of the European crises.

Rose Kennedy's datebook was filled with carefully penciled-in engagements for every day, weeks in advance. Since Joe represented the United States, they were invited everywhere. However, one event stood out. Rosemary and Kathleen had so much to do as they prepared for May 11, the day the two young women would be presented at court.

The *New York Times* reported on Rosemary's presentation to King George and Queen Elizabeth: "Mrs. Kennedy wore a gown of lace embroidered with silver and gold over white satin with a train of white tulle embroidered to match. Miss Rosemary Kennedy had a picture dress of white tulle embroidered with silver paillettes and worn over white satin with a train similar to her mother's."[10]

From left: Kathleen, Rose, and Rosemary in their gowns

Mrs. Kennedy wrote in her diary that very evening she felt like Cinderella. Rosemary's feelings must have surpassed her mother's!

Corisande, the well-known columnist of the *Evening Standard*, wrote, "Miss Rosemary Kennedy, one of the daughters of the American Ambassador, looked particularly well in her picture dress of white and tulle embroidered with silver." [11]

Rosemary was a knockout! Of the three hundred young women making their debut to the king and queen, she was one of only seven Americans. Rosemary and Kathleen *were* the United States.

Rosemary knew the pageantry's strict rules: When each young woman walked, the length between the gowns' trains had to be exactly the same. The young women were to bow to the king and queen two at a time. Because her father was the American ambassador, the reporters and photographers focused on the Kennedy sisters for the evening.

Training for the event, they practiced at the ballet barre, bending one knee nearly to the floor while keeping their backs perfectly straight.

Perhaps Rosemary's stomach clenched; her foot tapped next to her dressing table.

Will I curtsy correctly? Walk exactly as I was taught? Will I disappoint my family?

The gathering was the social event of the season. Reporters and photographers gathered from throughout the world.

King George, with Queen Elizabeth on his arm, entered the white and gold ballroom of Buckingham Palace at 9:30 p.m. as the band played "God Save the Queen," the country's national anthem. The king wore the uniform of a field marshal, including a tall dark hat with ostrich feathers hanging from the top. His suit coat was covered with medals; a gold stripe ran down the sides of his dark pants. He wore white gloves.

Rosemary dances with family friend Edward Moore

The *New York Times* described the queen as "glittering with diamonds . . . wearing a gown of silver lamé." [12]

The scene was straight from a fairy tale. Jewels, sequins, and chandeliers shimmered. The men standing at the back of the ballroom included Charles Lindbergh, who, like the others, wore velvet knee britches. Rosie's father stood out from the other men because he wore a suit, believing it unbecoming for an ambassador to wear the undignified breeches he considered more appropriate for young boys.

King George and Queen Elizabeth sat on a dais at the front of the room and the music began. The young ladies floated two by two through the majestic ballroom toward the royalty. Their satin gowns swished and their jewels sparkled. Many members of the royal family attended, as did the diplomatic corps and hundreds of English citizens.

Rosemary and Kathleen proceeded up the red carpet together, their heads held high. All eyes were on them as their names were announced.

Rosemary stood before the king and queen. She smiled, then curtsied perfectly.

She turned to leave . . . then . . . tripped.

The royal couple pretended nothing was amiss. No one in the crowd reacted. The music and the procession continued. There was no mention of Rosemary's slip in the avalanche of newspaper and magazine articles that followed.

Afterward, Mrs. Kennedy complimented both daughters.

When England entered World War II in September 1939, Joe continued as ambassador in London while most members of the Kennedy family returned to the safety of the United States. Rosemary stayed on in Hertfordshire, the countryside outside London, where she was happy. She enjoyed a close relationship with her father at that time, for she didn't have to share him with her siblings.

She wrote to him as follows in April 1940:

> *"Well Daddy . I feel honour because you chose me to stay*
> *.And .the others suppose are wild . . . .*
> *Much, Love,*
> *Rosemary*
> *PS I am so fond of you. And. Love you very much*
> *Sorry. To think that I am fat you. think) . . . "* [13]

While Rosemary was in Hertfordshire, she worked with young children at a Montessori School. She was enchanted by their wide-eyed reaction to the tales she read to them and the games she led of make-believe. Her whole outlook brightened when she discovered how she could be helpful to and admired by her small charges.

For Christmas 1939, Joe and his family reunited in the United States, but he chose to leave Rosemary behind in England, where she had settled in. Although some thought this proved coldness on Joe's part, leaving Rosie in England for Christmas spared her a trip home he considered too arduous for her.

During the spring of 1940, when Hitler seemed intent on invading England, Joe's friend Eddie Moore and his wife Mary brought Rosemary back to the United States.

In the next chapter of her life, Rosemary's problems deepened and worsened. Her behavior seemed uncontrollable and at times she showed incomprehensible anger. Her family was frightened for her.

Rosemary and Stella
In Their Twenties

"Hurry up, Stella! We're leaving for the dance!" cried her sister Florence.

Arnold drove Stella, Florence, and Al in their 1929 four-door Chevy sedan to another dance at Silver Lake Beach in Oconomowoc, ten miles from the farm. Stella rolled down the window to enjoy the warm summer breeze, a temporary relief from Wisconsin's humidity. Frogs croaked and fireflies twinkled in the darkness as the car bounced along dirt roads at a good thirty-five-mile-an-hour clip. For the night, Stella was free of farm chores, housework, and church duties.

In their 1920s-style frocks, with low waists and pleats, the women carried pocketbooks, and inexpensive beads swung from around their necks. Gene Austin's "Yes, Sir! That's My Baby" played while they visited the refreshment table.

"Excuse me," a young man said to Stella. "May we dance?"

"Yes, thank you," she said as the band struck up "Sweetheart Waltz."

The man glided Stella around as she counted in her head, *One-*

two-three, one-two-three. She had barely caught her breath when the fiddles began a rousing square dance.

"Yee-haw!" yelled some of the farmers, slapping their thighs. "Turkey in the Straw" began and a new partner grabbed Stella's hand for a dance. That was Friday night.

From left: Anita, Lucille, Stella, and Florence

For the Koehlers, Saturdays and Sundays were filled with local tennis matches, card games, and church suppers.

"I loved our card-playing and our dances," my aunt reminisced. "But I had *the calling.*"

"What's a calling?" I asked.

"It's a knowing deep in your soul," she said.

Once Stella understood she'd been called, she knew instinctively it was right. She couldn't *wait* to become a nun. "I promised the Blessed Virgin Mary I would pray the rosary every day so as not to lose my vocation."

At 11:30 one night at the dance hall, she set down her cup of punch, mortified. She had forgotten to pray! She knelt quietly in a corner and recited the rosary while the crowd around her danced the Virginia reel and a circle two-step.

Stella playing tennis, 1930s

At Boston's Yacht Club, Rosemary smoothed her hair and stood alone in the ballroom as Jack wrote his name on his sister's dance card. Jack was Rosie's favorite brother.

Both Jack and brother Joe were aware of Rosie's innocent nature and her beauty. They were expected to keep unsavory men away from her. But as a young woman, Rosemary seemed to understand her separateness from others, for she once asked her mother, "Why don't other boys ask me to dance?"[14]

In the fall of 1940, Rosemary unpacked her suitcase in a barren room at a convent school in Washington, D.C. No children surrounded her, eager to hear a story, as they had in England. Nor was there anything to remind her of her bedroom at Hyannis Port, like the sounds of ocean waves.

Eunice wasn't nearby to play tennis. Instead of swimming in the family's pool, Rosie would be going to mass in a somber chapel and genuflecting on hard wooden kneelers. After mass, nuns who were strict about discipline and rituals would tutor her in mathematics, English, and religion.

At night in her new school, Rosemary, now twenty-two, waited until the sound of the sisters' footsteps at last faded in the distance and the sisters' bedroom doors clicked closed. Rosie tiptoed to her window, opened it, lifted her skirts, and climbed over the sill. She reached her arms out for a nearby tree and slid down to the ground. She was free!

Tall and curvaceous, Rosemary had her mother's high cheekbones and her dark, thick wavy hair. She was striking. Her combination of beauty and diminished social and mental capabilities could have had disastrous consequences for a young adult like her, including sexually transmitted disease and pregnancy, both of which would have been especially grave for a young woman in a distinguished Catholic family. Because of their high profile in politics and society, the Kennedys couldn't risk the shame of such an occurrence.

Eventually, the nuns at the convent discovered that Rosemary had been sneaking out at night to meet men in taverns—men who were happy to give her attention, comfort, and sex. The sisters informed her father, who was horrified. She was unlike his other children. He had no idea how to protect her but insisted that she had to return to their Boston home immediately. At that time, a double standard was at work: Young men could experiment with sex, but if an unmarried woman did the same, she brought shame and dishonor to herself and her family.

The disgrace of pregnancy for a single woman could end the possibility of marriage or a career as well as associations with family, friends, and colleagues.

From the D.C. convent, Rosemary returned home a changed young woman. Having experienced a different kind of life that included fun and exploration, she wanted more freedom than her parents allowed.

She asked her mother why she was the only one who had a governess and why her younger sisters, and not she, could come and go as they pleased. Her mother said the arrangement was for her own safety.

It's conceivable that a mother-daughter conversation such as this one launched a tantrum that quickly spun out of control. Whatever the trigger, Rosemary's emotional outbursts became more frequent. Rose was shocked by her daughter's erratic and increasingly belligerent behavior. Rosie had been such a sweet child.

"In one traumatic incident during the summer of 1941, Rosemary, who was sitting on the porch at Hyannis, suddenly attacked Honey Fitz [Rose Kennedy's father], hitting and kicking her tiny, white-haired grandfather until she was pulled away." [15]

This violent rage was contrary to her normal disposition. She experienced physical seizures, and was soon diagnosed as having epilepsy.

Feeling desperate, the Kennedys searched for possible treatments. Joe learned of a new, supposedly state-of-the-art surgical technique called a prefrontal lobotomy. He suggested it to Rose, who asked Kathleen to find out more about the procedure.

Upon learning that patients often experienced extreme personality changes, loss of motor control and other functions following surgery, Kathleen said, "Oh, Mother, no, it's nothing we want done for Rosie." [16]

So the matter was dropped.

Or so Rose thought.

Rosie in her early twenties—gorgeous and vivacious

❦

"There's a dance at Silver Lake tonight!" cried Arnold. "Are you coming?"

"Yes," said Stella from the bedroom. "I'm changing right now!"

Though she was to enter the convent the following day, she and others planned to go out dancing that night. Except for her immediate family, she had told no one of her career plans.

She danced the beer barrel polka and afterwards drank a glass of punch with Anita and their neighborhood friends. Like Cinderella, who made a quick exit from the prince's ball when the clock struck midnight, Stella lost track of the time.

"I must go!" she suddenly said, putting down her cup.

"Why?" asked one fellow, urging her back onto the dance floor. "They'll play 'Turkey in the Straw' next, and we haven't done a square dance yet."

"I have to get up early in the morning. I'm going to the convent."

Everyone around her burst out laughing.

"Sure you are, Stella," said her dance partner. "Let's trot!"

"No, really," she said.

They all shrieked louder.

But the next day, because all clothing would be provided her at the convent, she packed her trunk with only a towel and a washcloth. Al loaded it into the car and settled into the driver's seat. Her parents rode along in the backseat, accompanying Stella on the way to Milwaukee. But first they stopped at Aunt Tilly's house in downtown Dousman. Aunt Tilly was married to Uncle Andrew, Kathryn's brother.

Aunt Tilly saw the car drive up in front of the house and came running out to meet them.

Stella poses on a country road, 1930s

Stella enters the convent

"I came to say goodbye," said Stella, getting out from the front passenger seat. "I'm going to the convent."

"No," said Aunt Tilly. "Don't tease me like that."

"I am," she said. "See my trunk?" She pointed to the back of the 1929 Chevrolet. The trunk was strapped right in front of the spare back tire. "There's the proof!"

Aunt Tilly fanned her face with her hand. It *was* true. Before Stella's parents could return home, the whole town of Dousman heard the news.

In 1936, when she entered the seminary, Stella was twenty-four, which was practically ancient for a woman intent in those days on becoming a nun. She was twenty-nine when she professed, or took her final vows.

She would face a new life of restrictions, some like those that confined Rosemary Kennedy. But unlike Rosemary, Stella Koehler had a choice about the shape her life would take.

Stella Becomes Sister Paulus

Before entering the chapel of Saint Francis Seminary, Stella's mother, Kathryn, pinned her hat onto her head. Stella and her sisters carefully attached black lace doilies to theirs. Kathryn had extra pins and tissues in her purse in case an unprepared female had a bare head emergency.

As the organ strains of "Nearer My God to Me" reverberated throughout the church and the St. Francis of Assisi Sisters choir sang in Latin, the bishop and altar boys proceeded down the aisle bearing the cross. The families of the novitiates stood, rising from their kneelers.

Two by two, the novitiates followed the bishop down the aisle to the altar. Stella seemed to float in the procession. Sunlight streamed through the stained glass window of *The Resurrection*, casting an iridescent rainbow over the altar.

Kathryn crossed herself. Perhaps the rainbow was a sign from Anita, the daughter she had lost a year before to tuberculosis. Stella had grieved for her closest sister, all the more so because it hadn't been possible for her to leave the convent to attend the funeral.

Stella at Profession of Vows with her father and mother (Harry & Kathryn)

On that same day, less than an hour's drive from Dousman, another brilliant rainbow appeared in nearby Oconomowoc, on the town's movie screen: the premiere of *The Wizard of Oz* on August 12, 1939.

Although the Koehler brothers were deeply moved by their sister's profession of faith, they eagerly anticipated the Milwaukee Brewers game later that day. They didn't have the money or time to attend the game at the county stadium, but they'd listen to it back at the farm on the radio in the barn.

Kathryn didn't care about movies or baseball. Experiencing both joy and sorrow, she wiped tears from her eyes with a handkerchief. When Stella took her vows, it was as though the Koehlers did too. Kathryn had already lost the daily closeness she had shared with Stella, and she worried about her daughter's lack of freedom within the convent.

When Paul chose the priesthood as his profession, Kathryn and Harry had felt only pride. Priests didn't take vows of obedience that obligated them to sequester themselves from their families. But Stella was allowed only one visit home a year, for five days including travel time. Phone calls were prohibited except in emergencies (letters were permitted).

Unlike Paul's vows, Stella's included poverty. The lifestyles of Paul and Stella differed greatly. Celibacy was the one vow they had in common.

As the organ music swelled and each novitiate took her turn at the altar, Stella's parents watched for her. She had spent six months as a postulant and two years as a novitiate, and the vows she was about to take were for life. When she reached the altar and stood in front of the bishop, Mother Superior exchanged Stella's short black veil for a longer one lined with stiff, white material reaching to her hips. A small woven crown of vines, with a single rose pointed toward the front, perched on top of the veil.

Stella's father, Harry, Stella, Father Paul (her brother) and Kathryn, her mother

"I, Stella Koehler, vow and promise to Almighty God, in the presence of the Blessed Mary ever virgin, Our Holy Father Saint Francis, all the Saints, and you, Mother General, to live forever in obedience, chastity, and poverty according to the Rule of the Third Order of St. Francis, and the Constitutions of the Sisters of the Third Order of St. Francis of Assisi, of Penance and Charity." [17]

The bishop anointed her with holy water. "In the name of the Father, and of the Son, and the Holy Ghost, I declare you a bride of Jesus Christ."

With those words, he slipped a gold band on the third finger of Stella's left hand. The gathered congregation began "The Prayer of Saint Francis":

"Lord, make me an instrument of your peace.
Where there is hatred, let me sow love;
Where there is injury, pardon;
Where there is doubt, faith . . .
Where there is despair, hope,
Where there is darkness, light,
And where there is sadness, joy . . . [18]

Stella had spent her childhood skating on Hattimer's Creek, dancing at Silver Lake Beach, and winning tennis tournaments. Her quiet, sequestered life in the convent must have seemed stark by comparison. At that time, before Vatican II, nuns were regulated by the chime of bells, paying penance by prostrating themselves on the floor in the shape of a cross, and by the once-a-year obedience cards that sent them to their next assignments.

Some women became sad or bitter; others simply left. But Sister Paulus completed her journey with love and joy intact. She shared both with Rosemary Kennedy when she became her caretaker.

Sister Paulus by the church's station wagon

Rosemary's Surgery

In 1941, unbeknownst to his wife and family, Joe Kennedy took Rosemary to be examined by Dr. Walter Freeman, a neurologist and psychiatrist who was also a professor at George Washington University. Joe had read about the doctor's successes in *Life, Time,* and *Newsweek* magazines.

Dr. Freeman's diagnosis of Rosemary was "agitated depression." [19] He claimed a lobotomy would not only relieve her of the rages she suffered but also render her happy and content.

The prestigious doctor, an imposing six feet tall, bore a professorial-looking mustache and beard. He assured Joe that a lobotomy was the best option available for Rosemary.

Joe said he wanted the doctor to proceed.

Dr. Walter Freeman

Why would a father agree to this drastic procedure for his daughter? In the early-and-mid-twentieth century, many people believed mental illnesses such as "agitated depression" were the result of a communicable disease. Others believed "bad blood" within a family could cause mental abnormalities. Still others were convinced that mentally ill people somehow contained the devil, an idea put forth long before by John Calvin and Martin Luther.

Whatever the cause, when it came to the mentally ill, fear was rampant. If those suffering from mental illness weren't hidden away, they were sometimes ridiculed, bullied, and abused.

Most treatments for brain disorders then hearkened back to the Middle Ages. For example, in so-called sleep therapy, patients were kept comatose with opium-type drugs for up to a month at a time, and were awakened only for brief daily periods so their feeding and toileting needs could be met.

Some physicians removed a patient's endocrine or thyroid gland, ovaries, tonsils, or teeth in hopes of stabilizing emotions. Males were sometimes castrated.

Some patients received horse blood through shots in their cerebrospinal fluid. Others were forced to inhale carbon dioxide during as many as 150 sessions. Sodium amytal, nicknamed the truth drug, got patients talking, but that did little good then—psychoanalysis and talk therapy weren't popular at the time.

Doctors who believed in the focal infection theory thought bacteria from cavities or bad tonsils caused mental problems. As a result, some patients were subjected to dental extractions and tonsillectomies.

In hydrotherapy, patients were subjected to rain douches or showers of water.

With electroshock therapy, an electric current passing through the patient's brain produced seizures. This was considered a breakthrough in the 1930s.

However, despite the many different methods used to relieve symptoms of mental illness, few if any were consistently or predictively effective.

With no good treatments available to them, people with mental disorders were regarded with repulsion. Many were hidden away in attics or locked inside institutions to prevent a family's social shame or its economic ruin. There were no government resources or volunteer organizations, as they are today, to provide financial or emotional assistance.

Doctors advised families to send the mentally ill to institutions, which, they said, could better care for them. And, once a family member was committed to those institutions, relatives were often told to never visit. The rationale for isolation was that family access would disturb the routines physicians believed necessary to improve the patient's health, for if a patient was reminded of his or her past emotional bonds, it would add to their emotional stress and cause further agitation.

According to an article in a 1938 *New England Journal of Medicine*, there was "one bed for mental disease for each bed for all other diseases in America." [20] Without government regulation, patients were often neglected and abused physically, emotionally, and sexually.

Institutions hired unskilled workers as caretakers, and paid them poorly to tend to patients' daily physical needs. It was difficult to find workers to fill these ungratifying positions, and desperate employers sometimes enlisted whoever turned up, including criminals.

Background checks were not part of the screening and hiring process. Because there was no system in place to follow up on an employee who harmed a patient, an abuser fired from one institution could move to a different city and be hired by an unsuspecting employer there.

Patients were restrained in unclean, dismal, poorly lit cells, with no fresh air and little hope for improvement. Many cycled downward. With the onset of the Great Depression, and later World War II, widespread overcrowding occurred, with criminals, alcoholics, drug addicts, indigents, and mentally ill patients all housed together.

Due to lack of funding and a disregard for the mentally ill, patients were sometimes fed only soup and cornmeal instead of nutritious meals. One attendant from a New Jersey state hospital reported, "I have seen coleslaw salad thrown loose on the table, and the patients expected to grab it as animals would . . . Tables, chairs, and floors are many times covered with the refuse of the previous meal." [21]

Starvation wasn't the worst ordeal residents endured. Overcrowding in old firetrap buildings was common. Restraints such as handcuffs, locks, straps, and sheets were used regularly. Administering sedatives or other behavior-modifying drugs was common. Beatings and murders were not rare events.

So when the lobotomy was embraced by some members of the medical profession in the late 1930s, it was because doctors were under extreme pressure to provide some relief to patients and their families. At the time, few experts believed mental illness could be treated effectively with psychiatry. Another treatment method was needed, and doctors around the globe were highly motivated to solve the problem. The competitive spirit among many physicians also fueled those who championed the latest procedures.

When Portuguese neurologist Egas Moniz began performing prefrontal lobotomies in 1935, he raced to publish his findings without thoroughly studying and assessing the after-effects. At age sixty, he was relatively old for a physician. He knew he didn't have much time to make his mark and thus felt a strong incentive to beat his rivals in discovering a "miracle cure" for brain disorders. It appears he had a healthy ego, too. At one point, he even went so far as to suggest to fellow physicians that they nominate him for the Nobel Prize.

In October 1949, Moniz was in fact honored with the Nobel Prize in Physiology and Medicine for his work with lobotomies. He won the award even though he had never operated on a single patient. Because he suffered from the chronic pain of gout, he directed other surgeons performing the procedure.

American neuropathologist and neuropsychiatrist Walter

Freeman met Moniz at a London neurology conference in 1935 and read an article he had published detailing his surgical success. Immediately upon returning to the United States, Freeman ordered two lucotomes—the thin instruments which contain an inner wire that surgeons rotate inside a patient's brain to destroy the nerve fibers during a lobotomy. Then he sought a neurosurgeon partner, and enlisted Dr. James Watts. Together they practiced on the brains in cadavers.

Freeman was not a surgeon but a professor of neurology at George Washington University, and well-known for his theatrics. In fact, Freeman's male students brought their girlfriends to his lectures to be entertained. With the audience assembled, he performed autopsies during which he held up various organs of the body "dribbling blood, so that students in the back row could see." [22] To demonstrate the ravages of dementia, he fed a patient from a baby bottle at the front of his lecture hall.

"Freeman thrived on the 'horror and fascination' that accompanied such demonstrations," wrote Jack Pressman, author of *The Last Resort: Psychosurgery and the Limits of Medicine*, "especially the publicity and the notoriety they engendered." [23]

By the end of 1936, Freeman and Watts had completed twenty operations. For subjects, Freeman searched sanitariums and taverns. His real expertise was public relations. At annual meetings of the American Medical Association, he "would stand by his exhibit and as people approached, he employed a clicker that made a sharp staccato noise. When the visitor stopped by his booth, he would begin to talk like a barker at a carnival. Then a crowd would gather and, before they moved on, they heard his story about the procedure's potential to provide patients dramatic relief from emotional tension, depression, and suicidal ideas. They were also shown his pre- and post-operative photographs, x-rays, and sketches of the typical lobotomy operation." [24]

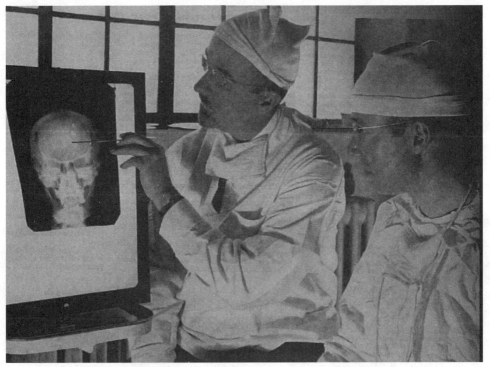

Dr. Walter Freeman, left, and Dr. James W. Watts study an X ray in 1941

Freeman shrewdly spread the word among the press. His so-called cure for many mental disorders made for good copy. His articles, replete with scientific errors, ran in popular national magazines: *Reader's Digest*, *Saturday Evening Post*, *Time*, *Newsweek*, *Harper's*, and *Life*. Headlines included "No Worse Than Removing a Tooth" and "Wizardry of Surgery Restores Sanity to Fifty Raving Maniacs." [25]

Until 1954, when chlorpromazine, or Thorazine, the first drug for schizophrenia and manic depression became available, lobotomies were still being touted as the best available hope for patients with serious mental illness.

Some patients actually improved with Freeman's drastic

surgical intervention. One suicidal woman said after her surgery that she experienced a feeling of peace and never felt depressed again. Some violent individuals were calmed enough not to be a danger to themselves or others in institutions.

Mostly, Freeman experimented on mentally ill patients who lived in state institutions. These dumping grounds housed patients who were considered to be "lost causes." Many patients had been abandoned by their families, so if Freeman and his assistant botched a case, no one cared or complained.

Freeman's research on his patients after surgery was woefully inadequate and his record-keeping and data were slanted to make him appear more successful than he actually was.

What about other doctors at the time? Didn't they become suspicious? Even today, we have an unwritten professional code where doctors don't speak out against other physicians. Given the desperation rampant in the field of mental health, they needed all the positive possible press they could get, and Freeman seemed to generate much of it.

By 1951, an estimated 20,000 lobotomies had been performed in the United States. The popularity of the surgery increased sharply in the early 1940s, but long-term effects were not known when Joe gave his consent for Rosemary's procedure in 1941.

When Freeman told Joe that Rosemary would benefit from the operation, he likely boasted of his success with his patient, Emma Ager, who like Rosemary, suffered from "agitated depression." He often showed before and after pictures of his patients, and he may have done this as a selling point to Joe as well. In the photo taken before her lobotomy, Emma looked miserable. In her post-op shot, Emma appeared relaxed and content. Dr. Freeman may well have noted Mr. Kennedy's keen interest in the photos as he told his prospective client that Emma didn't complain after her lobotomy. He'd adjust his wire rim glasses and say Emma was cheerful now, and had returned to her job after a two-month recovery.

Next Dr. Freeman might have given him a photo of a construction worker in the throes of depression and described his suffering: nervousness, worry, palpitation, throbbing in the head, fear of falling, and ideas of suicide. Then he'd display a picture of the same man in good health and tell Joe how the man, post-surgery, worked and lived a normal life.

Joe may have sat back in his chair to contemplate his daughter's condition. Rosemary's violent outbursts, her nightly wanderings, and his own desperate worry over her uncertain future clouded his mind. Then he stared at the "after" photographs. Would this surgery be the answer?

Dr. Freeman's positive outlook undoubtedly helped Joe make his decision. According to testimony by other patients and their families, Freeman exaggerated his claims and apparently discounted or forgot his failures.

In the fall of 1941, Dr. James Watts assisted Dr. Freeman in Rosemary's prefrontal lobotomy at George Washington University Hospital. Their procedure was well-established by then. Rosemary would be numbed with Novocain and mildly sedated before surgery began. It was important for her to be conscious so she could respond to Dr. Freeman's commands. She would feel little, if any, pain.

As nurses shaved the front of Rosemary's head, Dr. Watts and Dr. Freeman prepared for surgery. In this instance, Freeman assisted Watts by operating on the prefrontal lobe, the area of the brain behind her forehead. He participated without a medical license to do so.

By the time Dr. Freeman joined Dr. Watts in the operating room, Rosemary was reclined with her head resting on a sandbag. She was relaxed but still able to talk. Dr. Watts drilled holes into each side of her prefrontal lobe. He slid tubing from a two-and-a-half inch needle inside her brain. He then twisted a "blunt spatula, much like a calibrated butter knife," [26] upward inside her brain.

At this point, Dr. Freeman asked Rosemary to sing a song. As she sang, Dr. Watts continued to twist the "spatula." When she could no longer respond to their instructions, the doctors knew the lobotomy was complete.

⊰❀⊱

Lobotomies came to be known as the "surgery of the soul." [27] If a patient was agitated and violent before the operation, afterward it seemed as though his or her personality had been erased. It was not uncommon for a lobotomized patient, following surgery, to sit listlessly, staring straight ahead for hours.

In 1945, Dr. Freeman, on his own, experimented with another type of lobotomy. He used an ice pick to enter the patient's brain through the eye sockets. "The first ice pick came right out of our kitchen drawer and it worked like a charm," Dr. Freeman's son, Franklin, later recalled.[28]

This so-called transorbital lobotomy was considered an improvement over the surgery Dr. Freeman and Dr. Watts had performed on Rosemary because the patient came out with two black eyes instead of scars. Dr. Freeman himself liked this procedure because he could complete it in his doctor's office within ten minutes.

Dr. Freeman had little regard for the finer details of surgery, such as wearing a mask, draping the patient, or cleanliness. Dr. Watts disagreed with his lax attitude about such matters. Eventually, their different perspectives caused their partnership to break up. After Dr. Freeman began performing transorbital brain surgery, he traveled around the United States in a van he called his "lobotomobile," [29] which he used to demonstrate his techniques to hospital officials.

Faster than getting their teeth cleaned, patients could be

lobotomized. A surgical procedure that began as a last-resort treatment for schizophrenia and epilepsy was suddenly being used to treat commonplace ailments, including insomnia, tension, nervous indigestion, and headaches. Lobotomies were also advertised as a cure for homosexuality. Dr. Freeman even performed the surgery on teenagers who misbehaved and on wives who didn't like housework.

❄❉❄

Joseph Kennedy had doctors perform a prefrontal lobotomy on Rosemary without his wife's knowledge. It may seem unfathomable that a loving husband not include his wife in such a major decision. But in the Victorian era in which Joe and Rose were raised, men in the family held the power and women were supposed to obey. Joe was used to making decisions. He had suffered no real tragedies by then. Success had come relatively easy to him. He relied on faith and prayer to see him through adversity.

In the years after Rosemary's surgery, some accused Joe of wanting his daughter out of the way because her behavior was tainting the family's reputation and would hurt his career as well as the social and political prospects for his sons.

But when I talked to his grandson Anthony Shriver, he offered a different perspective on Joe's motives. "The experts in the field recommended [this procedure] to give her a more peaceful and productive life. He had a relentless desire for all of his children to *be* the best and to *give* them the best. He had a track record of being determined to give his children the best of everything. The goal was to enhance her life." [30]

Although Dr. Freeman and others touted the procedure as quick and easy, recovering from a lobotomy can be slow and complicated. A neurologist on the faculty of the University of California, Berkeley,

Dr. Steven Holtz, explained: "When you do any kind of operation, there is swelling around the tissue that has been damaged, and the swelling impedes the function of the nerve cells and wires that come from those nearby nerve cells. When the swelling recedes, those cells and structures can start working again." [31]

Rosemary had to relearn many basic skills: how to walk, how to follow simple directions, how to communicate, and finally with my aunt, how to go to the toilet. She was never again the energetic person she had been before her surgery.

"The frontal lobe is the pilot of your brain," said Dr. Holtz. "It controls your executive function, which directs everything. The theory behind it is essentially preventing the direction of impulses that were adherent. When one emerges from a lobotomy, one becomes docile, placid, apathetic, and devoid of affect." [32]

Rose Kennedy and the rest of her family did not learn of Rosemary's surgery for twenty years. Rose herself didn't see her daughter again until after her husband's stroke in 1961, which rendered him wheelchair-bound and incapable of speech; he communicated through gestures, grimaces, and grunts. Following his stroke, when the professionals administering Rosemary's welfare could no longer talk with Joe, they contacted Rose.

After Rosemary's lobotomy, Joe told Rose and his children that her behavior had worsened. Doctors advised that she be institutionalized, for her own good. She was to have no visitors, because they could disrupt and confuse her. Joe respected experience and knowledge; because physicians during this time probably advised him in this manner, he may well have assumed that the experts knew best.

What effect did the disastrous outcome of his daughter's surgery have on Joe? With no one to confide in, he must have suffered horrible guilt. Not allowing himself to experience any emotion, he would have buried it. Because Rose and Kathleen had flatly vetoed the surgery, Joe hid the truth from them.

Mrs. Kennedy was devastated to lose Rosie. She had spent countless hours tutoring and nurturing her, more time than she spent with any of her other children. Her namesake looked like her, wanted only to please her—and yet she had been whisked away and banished.

There was no doubt that the situation with Rosie had become serious.

"She had become very upset and angry; even violent. And they didn't have tranquilizers in those days," my aunt recalled.

Rose Kennedy displayed photos of all of her children in the living room of the family's Hyannis Port home. Most of the photos were in full, bright color. The photographs of Joseph Jr. and Kathleen, both of whom died in the 1940s, were in black-and-white.

So was Rosemary's.

Although many color photos of Rosemary were given to her, Rose never replaced the black-and-white picture. She presented to guests the picture that best captured Rosemary as a young woman, beautiful and full of promise.

Rosemary received no visitors during the bleakest years of her life.

One of the Koehler family friends became a cloistered nun in the early 1960s; her parents felt bereft that they would never see their daughter again. Cloistered sisters, enclosed within their convent walls, have no contact with the outside world. They devote their entire lives to devotional prayer and spiritual contemplation.

Although she loved being a nun, the daughter suffered a nervous breakdown while in the convent. During her recovery, she relapsed and doctors administered electric shock therapy on her. Her parents were told by her physicians not to visit her, because their presence would make her worse.

A full twenty years after this advice was given to Rosemary's father, doctors still prescribed this cockamamie theory to the parents of the Koehler family friend, the nun. Because they were dutiful play-by-the-rules and "Doctor-is-God" small-town Midwesterners, who were they to doubt such authorities? How many other patients and families have failed to question their doctor's advice? And at what physical and emotional price?

The nun's parents stayed home, tortured by worry and grief for their daughter. Their solace was prayer. However, they didn't suffer in silence. They shared their woes with our family, and we joined them in prayer and gave them emotional support, even though we couldn't be with their daughter.

Meanwhile, she yearned to stay within her beloved community as a nun, but she wasn't given the choice; she was told to leave. She returned home, greatly saddened by this forced spiritual and career change. However, she didn't let this setback derail her life. She attended school, and went on to have a successful career, marriage, and family.

Many years after her initial breakdown, she was diagnosed as being bipolar. Symptoms of bipolar or manic depression, a major mood disorder, may include being depressed and exhausted during one period of time, while exhibiting racing thoughts, insomnia, sudden talkativeness, and agitated behavior in another stage. Some people are "rapid cyclers" whose moods may change hourly, daily, or weekly. Others may have longer cycles, with extended periods of elevated or depressed moods. In addition to medication and therapy, stress reduction, exercise, and improved diet may help reduce or moderate symptoms.

My mother, Sister Paulus, and I once discussed Rosie's lobotomy and how Joe had kept Rosie apart from her mother and family for so long—a full two decades. "How could she have let him keep her away from *her own daughter*?" I asked.

My aunt was sympathetic to Mrs. Kennedy's plight. "She loved

Rosemary very much," she replied. "You had to live back then to realize how different the role of women could be within marriage and society."

"It wouldn't have been easy to have been a mother and wife back then," said Mom. "She was taught to accept what her husband said, for he was knowledgeable about those things. Mrs. Kennedy had been shown by her mother before her and by the vows she took to obey her husband."

As it would turn out, mental illness became the shameful secret that our own family would share with the Kennedys.

AUNT ZORA

During the summer of 1961, when I was four, Mom, Dad, and I took a train to Southern California to visit Aunt Zora, my mother's younger sister, and her family.

Aunt Zora seemed as exotic as her Croatian name. She moved with confidence, with a lilt and a sway, a style I later learned was flirtatious. She was model thin, and her fashionably short brown hair framed dark eyes.

My Aunt Dorothy, their youngest sister, told me my mother had been the real beauty when they were young and Zora rather plain. But men whistled at, and flirted with, Zora, and her datebook was always full. People thought my mom was stuck up because she was so shy and self-conscious, while Zora was outgoing and high-spirited. She knew how to have a good time.

The house Aunt Zora, Uncle Carlos, and my two male cousins lived in was a sprawling ranch with a fountain and pond in the front yard and a Hollywood-size swimming pool in the back. No one I knew was richer, luckier, or lived in more beautiful surroundings. Warm, sunny, and the perfect place for a seemingly perfect family!

Zora and her husband

Their stylish kitchen even had a dishwasher! Every piece of then-modern '60s' style furniture in her house looked as though it had just been moved from a show room floor. I felt like I was vacationing with a television family. I remember sitting on the edge of the couch, afraid that if I sat back further I would wrinkle the fabric.

Zora's second husband, Carlos, was a shadowy, exciting, handsome Italian who looked slightly scary. My aunt had divorced her first husband, considered a sin in the Catholic Church, so this was another carefully guarded secret. Even when I heard it discussed among the aunts, the actual word "divorce" was whispered. Uncle Carlos had a mysterious job that involved Las Vegas. Later, I learned he was a bookie who worked for the mob. He made a lot of money, at least compared to my dad, who worked at a non-union factory. Uncle Carlos' illegal dealings allowed his family to live in Rolling Hills, a luxurious suburb of Los Angeles.

This trip to California was the highlight of my young childhood. I built sand forts on the beach, danced in the salt water waves of the ocean, and sat on a real live donkey in Mexico. But the most memorable moment of all was eating cinnamon toast in Aunt Zora's kitchen. To this day, when I smell fragrant cinnamon, I remember Aunt Zora.

After our vacation, I recall Aunt Zora flying back and forth between Milwaukee and Los Angeles, and never staying long. Once, when my older cousin Bob picked her up at the airport, she came bearing $100,000 cash, hiding it from Uncle Carlos' nefarious gangster associates. When he did business with his mob friends, he drove an old beater of a car, so they'd assume he was broke. Meanwhile, she drove a brand new, bright-red Thunderbird while wearing one of her mink stoles.

I wouldn't see Aunt Zora again until a year or two later, probably 1965, when she moved with her two boys to a small, dingy apartment in Milwaukee. She'd left Uncle Carlos. Climbing slanted cement steps up to my aunt's apartment, my mother and I were met not with sweet cinnamon, but with smells of cooking grease escaping an open screen door.

Inside, a naked light bulb hung above us in the dark hallway; paint peeled off the walls around us. It was the first time I remember feeling the air filled with tension. My cousin John and I were hustled away to play. We crept back into the hallway, bringing a few toys with us. This would be the best spot to see and hear as much as we could.

I saw Mom in the kitchen remove money from her purse and slip it to her sister Zora without a word.

John and I tiptoed away from our toys and peeked around the stove to see them sit down at a red Formica table. Aunt Zora's hands shook as she held a coffee cup in one hand, a cigarette in the other. She wasn't the aunt I knew from California; relaxed, suntanned, and smiling. Now she stared vacantly into space, her brown eyes rimmed with dark circles.

Even though I was only seven, I felt desperation all around her and knew something was very wrong.

Mom rose and put out lit cigarettes in ashtrays scattered about the kitchen. "You must be careful or you'll burn down the apartment building," she said.

I felt a warm hand on my shoulder. Looking up, I saw my dad at my side. *Caught!* He led us back to our toys in the hallway, while he sat in the living room reading a newspaper.

John and I went through the motions of playing with his miniature medieval castle; the bridge over the moat moved up and down with a little chain. We didn't say a word to each other, straining our ears to hear what our mothers were saying to one another.

What was going on? What were they talking about?

Aunt Zora led Mom into the living room and motioned us

silently to the curtain covering the window. With a furtive glance toward us, Mom held John and me back with her hand. Aunt Zora stepped aside, drawing the curtains back a mere inch from the wall, allowing us to peer through the crack to the street below.

My mother was in front, so I couldn't see a thing.

What were we trying to look at anyway? And why didn't my aunt just yank open the curtains?

Somewhere, a water faucet dripped. My dad, standing beside me, leaned his weight forward and the wooden floorboards creaked.

No one had told my cousin and me to be quiet. But instinctively we knew. This was important. We were spying on someone.

"See?" Aunt Zora said to my mother.

Mom nodded. She turned to look at Dad. They shared a knowing look. They both had seen something out of the ordinary. Mom's eyes were wide and scared. Dad's face was serious. Normally when he looked this way, he'd kneel and pray. But for some reason, he didn't do so now.

Then Mom remembered John and me.

"Just peek," she said quietly. "Don't move the curtain."

She moved aside, and John and I took her place.

Two men sat inside a black car parked outside the apartment.

"When I go anywhere, they follow me," said Aunt Zora, her voice shaking. Her hand also shook as she pushed her unkempt hair from her face.

I frowned. Why were these men after my aunt? *Somebody please tell me.*

Mom read my face. "It's an unmarked car," she said. "The FBI is watching because of your Uncle Carlos' business."

Aunt Zora let the curtain close.

The crack of light disappeared.

By the summer of 1965, Aunt Zora became so ill John came to live with us. It felt like a gift for me. I had a playmate for the entire summer! We picked fresh vegetables from the garden and munched on carrots and lettuce. We became pirates, cowboys and Indians, witches and warlocks. We organized neighborhood softball games, climbed trees, had treasure hunts. And we read books for the public library's story-time club.

Due to space limitations and our family's meager budget, John's teenage older brother, Joseph, had to go to live with Uncle Nick and Aunt Marion in Milwaukee. I'm sure this bothered my mother because Joseph craved attention. She had a way with kids and certainly was aware that he had behavioral issues. Whenever he visited, the pair shared long talks as she worked in the kitchen.

I remember lying in bed one early morning, the window open and the breeze fluttering my white curtains, and hearing my mother's voice outside.

"Oh my heaven. Joseph, how did you get here?"

I popped my head up at my window to see him huddled on our backyard metal lounge chair, covered with nothing but a damp tee-shirt, jeans, and morning dew.

He stretched and yawned. "I rode my bike," he said as if kids did this every day on busy Milwaukee city streets, traveling 30 miles through pitch-black darkness on I-94—all after Uncle Nick and Aunt Marion had gone to sleep.

Joseph's discipline problems continued while living with Uncle Nick and would only be explained thirty years later with a psychiatric diagnosis: schizophrenia. Just like his mother.

Symptoms often include hallucinations, difficulty sleeping and concentrating, erratic behaviors, and paranoid beliefs, such as the persistent idea that people are trying to harm you or your loved ones. Although I didn't witness all these symptoms, I *heard* evidence of them.

The last time Aunt Zora came into our lives, I was twelve years old. It was nearly bedtime when a car pulled into our driveway, its wheels crunching on our gravel.

"It's a taxi," said my father, peering out the window.

"Oh no. Zora," said my mother.

A sob escaped my throat. I didn't want to see Zora at her worst; if she came to us, I knew she was desperate. She'd tear apart our family again; drain our finances and emotions. When would it stop? I ran to my room and hid behind my door.

"Only a night or two," I heard my aunt beg in a shaky voice.

I covered my ears so I wouldn't hear the tension in my parents' reply. *Please don't let her stay*, I prayed. *Hail Mary, full of grace. Please don't let her stay here. Hail Mary, full of grace.*

Too many times I had seen my parents give away their money to Zora, only to have her return a few days later for more.

"What is she doing with it?" wondered my Uncle Nick aloud. "Burning it?"

She turned family members against each other with her lies.

My mother's blood pressure rose, and she was forced to go on medication. My father stayed on his knees longer at night for his prayers. Whenever Mom experienced migraines, we tiptoed around the house until they passed.

I didn't know what was wrong with Aunt Zora, but I knew she was bad for us. I wanted her gone. We didn't seem to be doing her any good anyway, because we never solved her problems. She kept getting worse.

While crying in my room, I heard the commotion subside in the living room and felt the house shudder. The front door had closed.

I tiptoed down the hall and peeked into the living room. "Is she gone?"

"Yes," said my father.

"What happened?" I was older now. I needed to know more.

"Your father paid the taxi driver to take her back to Milwaukee,"

85

said Mom, rocking back and forth in her rocking chair, fast and furious. "She was angry, but I couldn't let her stay here."

Fresh tears flowed from my eyes. I was so relieved.

"We can't seem to do anything for her," said my mother. She sounded so sad and so tired.

My father sat down. He shook his head. He, too, grieved. Neither of them had come up against anything like Zora before.

For me, it was easier to pretend Aunt Zora didn't exist. I could push her out of my mind.

Before mental illness appeared, Rosemary had been beautiful, lively, and full of warmth and gaiety—just like my aunt. When she disappeared from the Kennedys' lives, did they shut her out of their thoughts, too?

Later, when I was an adult, I brought up Zora's evening visit with my mother.

"I was so relieved when you sent her away," I told her.

"What?" she said. "I thought you wanted her to *stay*! I thought you were upset with me because I was cruel."

"No!" Now it was my turn to be shocked. "I knew she was destroying our family and everything she came near. She wore you down. She wore us all down. We couldn't have stood any more episodes. You were right to do what you did."

"Oh my," said my mother faintly. "All these years I thought . . ." Her words drifted off.

"I'm so sorry you didn't know," I said.

Silence and guilt: destructive behavior in any family.

Once, after I married in 1981, I returned home to Wisconsin with my husband to visit my family. My Aunt Mary held a backyard gathering with my mother's family.

"Your Aunt Zora would love to see you," Aunt Mary said, apparently having heard from her. Zora, living in an apartment, seemed to be holding her own.

I thought back to the tumultuous times when Zora flew back and forth from California to Wisconsin; a time when she couldn't help but drain the resources of everyone around her. When drama reigned, lies flew back and forth. I envisioned Aunt Zora now, holding a suitcase, standing on the doorstep of my California home.

"Tell Aunt Zora that I'm sorry, but I can't," I answered.

I never saw Aunt Zora again.

My cousin Ellen did. They were both at a shopping mall. Zora was thin as usual, and clean. Ellen called her name and said, "Your son has a daughter. You have a grandchild!"

"I have no son," she replied. "I am not *that* woman. I am not who you think I am."

I am not that woman. Perhaps she didn't remember that woman anymore. Perhaps she had never wanted to be her.

"I will leave their picture here for you to keep," Ellen said. She left the photo beside her on a bench.

Ellen, surprised Zora had denied the existence of her own son and grandchild, returned an hour later to find Zora gone but the photo still there.

I am not who you think I am. This reveals some of the deeper hardships of the mentally ill and their loved ones. Zora's mind was so troubled that she distanced herself from parts of her life that should have brought joy and comfort. We really didn't know her at all inside her illness. Sadness crept over me that we couldn't learn more.

Relatives raised Zora's children, and there hadn't been any contact between the children and their mother since they were young. Maybe it was easier for Zora to wipe away her past and become someone else. After all, we had all but erased her from ours.

A few years ago, I mentioned my Aunt Zora to my Koehler cousin, Mary, and she said, "Who? I've never even heard her name before."

Aunt Zora and Rosemary.

Two women missing for years from their family histories.

CRAIG HOUSE

After Rosemary's lobotomy in 1941, Joe Kennedy sent her to Craig House, in Beacon, New York, to go under the care of its director, Dr. Clarence Jonathan Slocum, who had purchased the General Howland and Henry Winthrop Sargent estates in 1915 and converted them into a sanitarium. In 1935, *Fortune* magazine chose Craig House as one of five in the country to profile. Craig House, it said, offered treatment, amenities, and atmosphere suitable for the wealthy.

Three hundred and fifty acres of lush grounds were filled with ginkgo, oak, and weeping beech trees put in by famed horticulturist Henry Winthrop Sargent. Two large Victorian manors, as described by *Fortune*, contained "ornately carved dark wood, a red and gold Chinese hallway, a pipe organ, [and] a conservatory with huge royal palms." [33]

The manors contained a dining room, libraries, and indoor recreation areas.

A mixture of large and small buildings containing suites and cottages, two gatehouses, a club house, and stables were scattered throughout the grounds. Rosemary lived in a gatehouse on the

Sargent estate. There were no wards or semi-private rooms. "Each patient has a private room and bath. The majority of quarters have a living room adjacent to the bedroom."[34]

Since Rosemary's post-lobotomy abilities were severely limited, she couldn't take advantage of the tennis courts, golf courses, baseball field, heated swimming pool, or the lake for skating. Her life narrowed to her quarters: one bedroom and one bath, with a small living area and kitchen. None of her family members ever visited.

Dr. Slocam didn't believe in psychoanalysis, so his "practical psychotherapy"[35] included his friendly doctor-patient relationship and occupational therapy such as arts and crafts, woodworking, weaving, etc., and hydrotherapy—a "douche of hot and cold water alternately applied,"[36] sitz baths, and "warm shallow baths that cleanse the perineum."[37]

"In our plan for treatment, we aim to give the patient as much freedom and personal liberty as is consistent with giving proper care," wrote Dr. Slocum in an undated letter.[38]

With no locked doors or windows, other patients freely roamed the estate for exercise and socialization. Each of the fifty-some patients' private attendants took care of their physical needs, dined with them, and played games with them. Other patients were taken on outings, such as going to the movies or shopping, but for safety and privacy, Rosemary was not.

The left side of Rosie's body had been partially paralyzed by the lobotomy. Her head tilted, frozen near her left shoulder. The fingers of her left hand became gnarled and useless. The sparkle faded from her eyes. She was lethargic and incontinent. She couldn't talk and relied on grunting, screaming, and shrieking to communicate with others.

Rosemary gradually relearned simple daily-care activities: walking, brushing her teeth, putting on a sweater, and opening a door. She slowly recalled some words, but she did not enunciate well, and many of her sentences made sense only to her. She didn't regain all basic toileting skills until my aunt became her full-time caregiver at Saint Coletta, in Jefferson, Wisconsin, once she was allowed a more normal life around people.

The lobotomy had not eased her temper tantrums. Her outbursts were worse than ever and she was so strong and volatile that *two* guards had to accompany her whenever she visited the doctor. She also required two attendants in her living quarters.[39]

Scenery-gazing from the automobile must have been a welcome diversion for Rosie. The thriving landscape afforded her a lovely drive while ensuring her privacy. Her father's orders insisted that Rosemary not be seen by anyone in public. Doctors told Joe her violent and temperamental behavior would worsen if family members visited her. So she had no guests.

For the Kennedy family, it was as though Rosemary no longer existed, which was how society treated the intellectually challenged at that time. Rosemary was missing from the lives of her parents, siblings, and other family members.

In dealing with Rosemary-related feelings and emotions, the Kennedys relied on the power of faith and ritual: attending mass, reciting the rosary, and praying. Religious ritual anchored them in a way the unpredictable world could not. It provided them a solid foundation—and perhaps the strength to survive the tragedies ahead.

While living at Craig House from 1941 until 1949, Rosemary went without the prayerful life she had always known. Her parents and siblings had the solace of their shared faith and the comfort of one another, and their belief Rosie was in the best place for her condition. Rosemary had neither faith nor comfort—nor hope.

Her life would take another dramatic turn in 1949 when her father decided to move her.

There was evidence Rosemary was being sexually abused at Craig House.

UNCLE NICK

Although I knew my mother's brother suffered from depression, I didn't understand what it meant because Uncle Nick always talked, smiled, and acted naturally at family gatherings. He was my mom's favorite sibling. He had a generous personality, deep brown eyes, balding head, and an affable smile. Though he was depressed, he hid it well.

What the heck was depression anyway? I wondered when I first heard about it as a teen. *Was it feeling like not talking to your best friend after a fight? Of not getting the right class you signed up for in college? When a boy you like doesn't like you back?*

My mother and her six siblings grew up placing cardboard inside their shoes when their soles wore out. She and my Uncle Nick and their brother and sisters were lucky to find a sparse bone to throw in their watery soup at night and went to bed with growling stomachs.

Nick, Bob, Al, Ann, and John

In the 1930s of small town Aurora, Minnesota, wood shop classes were basic requirements for middle and high school boys, while cooking and sewing were considered graduation essentials for the girls.

While attending school, Nick paid special attention to the mouthwatering scents of baked-from-scratch bread, simmering meaty stew, and chewy chocolate chip cookies as they wafted through the school's halls.

So Nick waltzed into the principal's office. "I want to take Home Economics," he announced.

The principal had never encountered a boy willing to enter an all-girls' class before.

"Whatever for?" asked the bewildered man.

"Can't a guy become a chef?" asked Nick.

Without a good reply for that one, the principal allowed him to enroll.

The first day he cooked and feasted on roast chicken was the first day he had a square meal in a long time. Nick bore the taunts of "sissy" from the other boys at school with equanimity; blackened eyes and a bloodied nose were fine if they were the only price to pay for quelling hunger pangs.

At the age of twelve, Nick had been the smallest guy in school, and so the old wife's tale about cod liver oil's miraculous ability to stimulate growth motivated him to dutifully swallow a spoonful of the ghastly-tasting stuff every day. By the time he graduated from high school, he was nearly six feet tall; in my mother's eyes, he stood even taller. His straight shoulders showed new confidence; his warm, shy smile engaged my mother, whose own self-esteem never was very great.

After he worked in the Civilian Conservation Corps and put himself through college, Nick got a job teaching wood shop to high school students, got married, and had a child. Because the rest of the family muddled along, earning low-income wages, Nick felt privileged receiving a higher, steady salary because he was the only sibling with a college degree. On several occasions, he presented gifts to various family members who he knew were in financial need. However, he never told his wife about his contributions. We felt sad he didn't have a truthful, happy marriage.

In fact, Nick wasn't really happy at all. In public, he came across as a nice enough man, content with his life. But at home, the façade fell. To overcome his depression, he took amphetamines, which caused him to twitch and shake. But without the drugs, he'd sink so low he couldn't function.

He and his wife didn't talk most of the time. Their daughter, Ellen, mediated between them. For most of her life, she served as their go-between, the apex in this odd triangle. And though they didn't talk much, they stayed together even after Ellen grew up and left home.

Uncle Nick and his wife Marion

When Nick got older, other health problems developed—congestive heart failure and cancer. A grandchild arrived. She was everything to him, but her presence wasn't enough to drive the depression away.

My aunt heard the gunshot coming from the bedroom.

One of my mother's sisters called to tell me. I broke the news to my mother.

Later, when lunching with one of my Koehler aunts, she said, "I read the obituary of your uncle. It didn't say how he died."

Pause.

I am my mother's daughter. No one had to tell me to keep *this* secret.

"He had cancer," I said.

A truth . . . and yet a lie.

When my uncle pulled that trigger, my son was nine.

"What happened?" my son asked me, after I sobbed into his

father's arms and calmed down enough to talk.

"Uncle Nick was very sick—so sick—and he was very sad. So he chose to end his life with a gun."

Once the trauma of the event passed, I made sure my son understood our family history and what options were available for those struggling with depression.

Silence and mental illness are not a very effective combination.

❧❀❧

As I tell this story, my mother and her siblings have passed on, but guilt surrounds each word I write. *These are family secrets.*

Nick's depression hampered him all of his life; Zora's schizophrenia and manic-depression (schizoaffective disorder) symptoms came on during her early forties. Eldest and youngest sisters Ann and Dorothy suffered from depression too. *Four out of seven siblings* were afflicted by mental illness.

During traumatic events in my Aunt Ann's life, such as when her son, Bob, joined the army, or when her daughter left for nursing school, Ann took to her bed.

"She's tired all the time," said my mother after we spent time at her house.

Why is she so tired when she never does anything? I wondered. I noticed her husband, my Uncle Frank, wearing an apron as he dried the dishes. He went to work *and* did the chores around the house. I didn't understand how exhausting it was to battle the symptoms of depression.

But other times, Aunt Ann functioned normally, as when she prepared and served elaborate Thanksgiving dinners. After she recovered from her husband's death, she worked outside the home, and even joked about spending eight hours on her feet while in her seventies. That couldn't have been easy for her. In her eighties and nineties, she suffered from dementia, but a flash of sharp wit occasionally shined through.

The author (center) naps with cousins after a Thanksgiving dinner

When my mother's youngest sibling, Dorothy, who lived in Southern California, needed elder care, I stepped in. Suffering from chronic pain, she found herself developing the symptoms of depression. Did she have it all of her life? Because she had lived far away from us and this illness hadn't been discussed, we didn't really know.

I sought out my mother's other sister, Mary. "Why was your mother sick and in bed all of the time?" I knew that their mother, my grandmother, who died in the 1940s from a stroke, was never around to take care of her seven children because she was sick in bed. But no one seemed to know why. Might this be the mystery disease?

"Could she have suffered from depression?" I asked her.

"I don't know," she said.

Mary was the one sister who didn't keep secrets well. If there was a secret here, she didn't know it. No one knew why their mother took to her bed so often. They didn't know her symptoms. Depression is a disease where symptoms often are not visible.

I received a letter from Uncle Nick's wife a week before he died. He refused to see his doctor and she wrote, "When he gets bad enough, he'll ask for help."

In his last weeks, no longer concerned about his physical appearance, he stopped shaving. His wife's letter said she and Ellen were at a loss as to what to do. We were all so uneducated about mental illness, we didn't know these symptoms were clues. Neither did he. He searched for a solution other than a prescription.

He took his life a few days after Thanksgiving. After his death, as I sat in church singing Catholic hymns, a flood of tears came on. During a holiday call to Sister Paulus, I accidentally broke down and confessed the truth to her.

I betrayed the secret. Aghast, I begged her not to tell a soul.

"Oh, E-liz-a-beth," she said, drawing out the syllables of my name in her soft, lilting tone. "No one has to know this. And no one will judge the poor man. God will love and forgive him. He is with God *now*."

It was as though the Catholic Church itself had spoken and released the gates of heaven to my uncle. Years of being told that suicide would permanently block heavenly redemption suddenly made me realize not only that I was grieving my uncle's death, but subconsciously *I was worried about his afterlife.*

Me. An adult who did not believe in a vengeful God, but one who is all-loving, still had visions of hell burned into my consciousness.

Me. Who proudly claimed to be a Cafeteria Catholic, never to be concerned about Catholic judgment again.

Me. A feminist Catholic, who claimed not to be affected by those old-fashioned beliefs, really was ingrained after all—a traditional Catholic to my core; somehow, Sister Paulus' love embraced this anxiety and eased it for me.

❧❀❧

In 1941, Rosie's treatment options were few, and it didn't seem as though modern medicine helped Uncle Nick very much in the 1980s and '90s. A friend of mine who suffers from depression today says it's as if there's "a big black hole" inside you and there is "no way out."

This friend keeps her depression a secret.

For her, and for many others, significant stigma still remains.

ROSIE AT SAINT COLETTA

Joe picked up the phone. At the other end was Boston's Archbishop Richard Cushing, who was recommending a good place for Rosemary. Joe and Cushing had been friends for years. The archbishop told him about Saint Coletta, a home for the mentally retarded in southeastern Wisconsin. It was run by the Sisters of Saint Francis of Assisi, and there could be no safer place for his daughter. The nuns who would be in charge of her care at the convent embodied the virtues of purity, goodness, and faith.

Joe probably traveled to Jefferson, Wisconsin, to view the farm, school, and dorms that stood alongside Highway 18 in the small country town, as he arranged the building of a ranch-style home there for Rosemary. Surrounded by a forest and a wide expanse of grass, three adult residential buildings, collectively called Alverno, lay a quarter mile north of the school. Near the Alverno dorms was Rosemary's home, called Saint Clare Cottage. There, she would live with two nuns for the rest of her life.

Alverno buildings at Saint Coletta

By the time Rosemary moved to Saint Coletta, its seventy-two sisters, twenty-plus educational and medical staff members, and handful of lay employees ran a school and provided care and vocational training for more than four hundred residents. Students raised beef cows, dairy cows, and chickens; grew vegetables; and maintained a cherry and apple orchard.

Rosie settled in Saint Clare Cottage and though she was well loved by the sisters, she still exploded with angry tantrums. Her father, mindful of prevailing 1940s psychiatry, admonished the nuns to keep Rosemary away from people. She should see no one and no one should see her. For Rosie, there would be no socializing in public—no connections to the outside world.

Rosie's life began to change dramatically with my aunt's arrival at Saint Clare Cottage in 1960. It was as if Sister Paulus had been born for this role. My aunt bonded quickly with Rosie.

Sister Paulus walks the path in front of the cottage

"She was difficult at first," my aunt said, recalling their first year together. "She had a lot of anger in her."

Sister Paulus knew instinctively how to relate to Rosie. While having lunch with them one day, I noticed that when Sister Paulus made eye contact with her, they shared a smile that lit up Rosie's eyes.

"Notice how she talks to you with her eyes?" Sister Paulus asked.

I nodded.

"Her eyes tell you what she is thinking and feeling every moment," said my aunt.

"I like the way you are using your fork, spoon, and napkin," she said to Rosie.

Rosie's eyes shone. Sister Paulus squeezed her hand. She

didn't change her voice when she talked to Rosie but treated her as an equal. The more Sister Paulus spoke in a gentle voice to Rosie, complimented her, and sustained eye contact with her, the softer and more loving Rosie became.

In 1961, the administrators of the Alverno residences assigned Sister Paulus to be in charge of more students in a group home. She moved into Alverno's women's dorm and later became Mother Superior at Saint Coletta's. The new separation from Rosie proved difficult for both of them.

It wasn't until 1968 that Sister Paulus was reassigned as Rosie's caretaker. For both Sister Paulus and Rosie, it was a joyous reunion. Although they had continued to interact frequently during their years apart—Sister Paulus chauffeured Rosemary everywhere—their connection hadn't been the same as when they'd been together full time.

Sister Paulus and Rosie enjoy a meal

"Why didn't you tell them you didn't want to leave Rosie?" I once asked my aunt.

"I took my vows: poverty, chastity, and obedience. Obedience means I do not question decisions made for me," she explained.

As a girl, I couldn't understand the life of a nun. It took me many years of reflection to fathom my aunt's commitment to, and passion for, this selfless life. But the years of quiet contemplation and servitude drew her closer to the spiritual happiness she loved.

Sister Paulus with the author on a family visit

After Joe Kennedy's stroke in December 1961, Rose Kennedy and the rest of the family discovered Rosemary's whereabouts and the strict rules Joe had set in place. Mrs. Kennedy was shaken by what she learned about her husband's edicts. Although she grieved for her wheelchair-bound husband, she was shocked by his beliefs. Rosie's safety had been an issue, of course—Rosemary was part of the rich and famous Kennedy family. But she was convinced that Rosemary deserved a more fulfilling life.

Rosie stands in front of her cottage

Rose understood her daughter needed to experience life in the world, so she called the Mother Superior who preceded Sister Paulus and told her to allow the nuns to take Rosemary shopping, out to restaurants, and to social outings. No longer sequestered, Rosemary began living a broadened life. This is when we began visiting Rosie, probably during early 1962. I was four to Rosemary's forty-three. She became accustomed to interacting in new settings with a variety of people. And, as might have been predicted, her behavior improved.

When she drove the car around to pick up Rosie and the other nuns, Rosie jumped up and down, Sister Paulus recalled. "Go! Time to Go!" Rosie would say.

Sister Paulus would respond with a laugh. "She sure loves a change of scenery, doesn't she?"

Rosie's outings were so pleasant, she couldn't *wait* to ride in the car, and she clamored to be first out of the Saint Clare Cottage. She particularly enjoyed window-shopping and would gaze blissfully at brightly colored clothes and accessories on display.

"Come along, Rosie," encouraged Sister Paulus. "We're going to a restaurant."

Rosie obeyed, walking faster. If there was one thing she enjoyed even more than window-shopping, it was dining out. It was a treat to eat out, though the nuns never took her to fancy places. They dined out on simple, good food.

When Rosie visited my family's house with Sister Paulus, she lit up and clasped her hands together, understanding that we were as excited to see her as she was to see us. If we met her and my aunt at a restaurant for a meal, Rosie would whisk her napkin from the table to her lap, demonstrating that she was ready to eat now.

As her life became less restricted, her tantrums waned.

Rosie stands in front of the field across from her cottage

When Rose Kennedy visited Saint Coletta for the first time, Rosemary and two nuns met her at the Milwaukee airport. Rose fingered her pearls as she departed the airplane. If she was lost in thought, it was understandable. She hadn't seen her daughter in twenty years. Would Rosemary even remember her? Rose believed she herself hadn't changed all that much in the past two decades— she even fit into the gown she had worn when her daughters were presented to King George and Queen Elizabeth.

When Rosemary saw her mother, she ran to her. The nuns quickened their pace, their dark robes flapping after them. Mrs.

Kennedy opened her arms in greeting as Rosie raised her arms, but the reunion quickly took an ominous turn. Rosie beat her mother's chest with her fists, shrieking with a primordial, *"AAAARRRRRCK!"*

The nuns tore Rosemary away from her shaken mother.

The lobotomy had not erased the past twenty years from Rosie's memory. She knew her mother had not been with her when she needed her most.

⊰⊱

"Hi, Rosie!" I said as she wiggled and happily bounced her feet when my parents and I came to see her.

The scent of roses hung in the air like perfume. The vivid red and yellow flowers lined the picture windows inside and out. They were her favorite blossom as well as mine.

She stopped shuffling her greeting cards and offered me her hand as though she were royalty.

Perhaps her continual card shuffling kept her thin fingers agile. Right before she relaxed into her chair and began listening to music, or as the television played in the background, she would move bright, colorful greeting cards from one hand to another. Some were sent from friends and relatives; others were gathered and saved for her. Sister Paulus varied them so she had a rotating collection to view and play with.

"Suffle ex day lux or ip a duh match them is good but darabem tang dor dittor am Europe!" she said.

Despite her garbled words and tangled syntax, her rapid-fire pace and her escalating volume signaled that whatever she was saying was important. And one word was perfectly clear: *Europe*. It was her favorite topic to discuss with me.

Rosie shuffles her greeting cards

Rosie's eyes sparkled; her skin glowed. I was sure she was telling me the fairy-tale-come-true story of how she and her family had traveled overseas—and about the night she made her debut before the royalty of England. Or maybe she was recalling how she and Eunice had traveled alone across Europe when she was eighteen and Eunice sixteen.

Soft brown and naturally curly hair framed Rosie's face. Even though her head tilted at an awkward angle and she made nervous hand-washing movements, she was still striking. Rosie was as tall as her mother was petite. They both shared the Fitzgerald bone structure, and her fair complexion was dotted with freckles. Rosemary reminded me of actress Patricia Neal.

As I held her hand, I told her, "Your fingers are so long and elegant. You could have been a pianist."

"Zelf em alp Europe!" she said. "Red and she upure the baby. But *she* upda piano." Rosie always referred to herself as *she*, not I.

Sometimes when my parents and I visited Saint Coletta, Sister Paulus brought Rosie and us next door to the dorm's recreation room. Rosie tapped her feet to music from the record player while other residents played games or talked.

"Will you dance with me?" I asked her.

Her wide smile gave me the answer and I grabbed her hands. We were off! Swaying and swinging to the rhythm, Rosie and I shared a special moment together. Sister Paulus, Mom, Dad, and the residents clapped when we finished. Rosie's eyes glowed, enjoying the attention. I bowed gallantly to Rosie and she laughed, her eyes twinkling. Did she remember dancing with her brothers at the balls they once attended together?

I loved visiting Rosie every month or two. I was delighted by the way she bounced with excitement to greet me and couldn't wait to tell me a story. She loved desserts as much as I did and let me play with and cuddle with her dog, Lolly.

At the time, seven of my father's nine siblings were still living and they, too, visited my aunt and Rosie occasionally. But most of my aunts and uncles had children and their lives were hectic. I was an only child, and it made sense that my father made an effort to visit Sister Paulus frequently—she had devoted so much time and energy to helping raise him.

The author and Sister Paulus on a visit

The author with her mother and father at one of three Alverno buildings

As a child, I skipped through Rosemary's house, with its spacious living room and large picture windows, looking out at pine, birch, and maple trees. I twirled in the center of the wood-paneled living room, my dress flying out around me as Rosie laughed, delighted. Residents waved as they strolled by on the quiet road between Rosie's house and a cornfield behind a white picket fence. Rosie and I would wave back in reply.

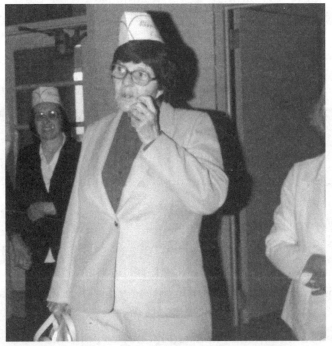

Sister Paulus and Rosie visit the Rippon Cookie Factory

My favorite room in her cottage was a large one, which served as both a dining area and den. It was here that the familiar faces of Ted, Eunice, and other Kennedys gazed back at me from photos perched on the bookcase and desk. The nuns' hand-crocheted doilies gave the room a cozy feeling, and religious artifacts dotted the walls.

A hall led from the dining area to the bedrooms and a bathroom. Two nuns slept in tiny, separate rooms, with closets that could accommodate only two habits. The sisters-in-residence shared a bathroom.

Another small room became a Kennedy guest room. The largest bedroom was Rosemary's; it faced the front of the house and had an adjoining bathroom.

One summer day, Sister Julaine, another nun who cared for Rosie, led my parents and me to the backyard of Saint Clare Cottage.

"They're swimming," Sister Julaine said. Her curly gray hair poked out from her short veil. A hard worker, she was known for her housekeeping skills, but she didn't have a close relationship with Rosie.

Rosie and Sister Paulus splashed delightedly in the above-ground pool. They both wore swimming caps and looked adorable. Rosie's freckled complexion shone in the sunshine. She smiled widely and yelled unintelligible words to us in a friendly greeting. My aunt's high cheek bones and clear skin highlighted her beauty and strength.

"Why, Elmer! Helen! Elizabeth! Do you want to come in for a swim?" Sister Paulus asked. "We have some extra suits if you need them." She knew I loved the water, too. "Usually Rosie and I swim in the big pool, but the weather was so warm, we decided to have a dip in here today."

The Kennedys had donated money to build an Olympic-sized pool for the entire community inside one of the Alverno buildings. The pool, named the Sister Anastasia Memorial Natatorium for a dedicated Franciscan sister, was Rosie's favorite place to be. Sister Paulus and Rosie swam in the indoor pool year-round. But today, Rosie smiled as she showed off her dog paddling skills to us in her backyard's outdoor pool.

"Good swimming, Rosie!" said my mother. "We'll take a pass on joining you, but please continue your swimming."

We wandered through the yard. "It's beautiful here," said my mother.

My father bent over out of habit and pulled a weed from the garden, which was filled with a colorful patchwork of peppers, cucumbers, tomatoes, and corn. I breathed in the scent of freshly mowed grass. Of all the scents that mingled at St. Coletta, my favorite was the sweet perfume of the yellow, red, and white roses brightening the house.

After my aunt and Rosie finished their swim and changed clothes, we sipped lemonade in the cottage's cool living room.

"Rosie is such a good helper," said Sister Paulus. "She washes the vegetables with me so I can chop them. And when we make soup, she stirs it." Rosie beamed.

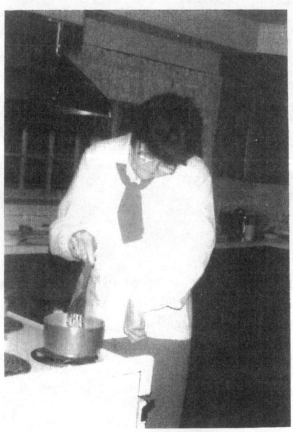

Rosie stirs a pot of soup

"The cutest thing of all is when we finish making her bed in the morning," added my aunt.

"Cute?" said my father. "Making a bed is cute?"

"She finishes by swinging her frilly pillow on the bed with a little lilt. Whee!" With the word "lilt," Sister Paulus swung her hips and one hand. I imagined a drumbeat accompaniment. We laughed and so did Rosie. She understood my aunt's humor!

Rosie makes her bed

When she didn't like someone or if she didn't get her way, Rosie could misbehave like a stubborn child. She wasn't fond of one of her caretakers and called her "the chauffeur" or "the maid." If that nun turned the television on so she could watch a program, Rosie stood in front of the set, blocking the view. She'd say, "Don't like that maid."

Once, when my uncle, Father Paul, brought another priest to

visit Rosie and Sister Paulus, the two men sat down at the dining table for lunch. Unfortunately, the other priest took a seat at the head of the table, in Rosie's usual chair.

"Don't like that man in black," she said throughout the meal. Rosemary *did* like her routines. She knew her place in her own home.

Sister Paulus and Rosie entertain guests during Christmas

Rosie's nephew, Anthony Shriver, loved Rosemary's home too. "It was a great experience for me as a young man to sleep in a tiny room with a desk and a chair. It was a calming environment and a refreshing experience. There was a kindness and a sweetness to Saint Coletta's. I went to chapel, met all of the nuns, and broke bread. Life was a great gift with Rosemary. I grew up in a hectic family with expectation and determination. Rosemary was a different kind of

Kennedy. Her home was a reflection of her lifestyle. It was calming and relaxing."

Rosie occasionally played miniature golf on the course next to her house. She wasn't passionate about the game, as she was for swimming, and she needed coaching. She met daily with the men and women who lived next door and they communicated by clasping hands, smiling, and talking. Although she didn't have a particular best friend, she conversed warmly with them, and they with her, in a language others couldn't understand.

The men and women who lived in the dorms next door never cared that Rosie lived in her own house. They treated her as an equal and never showed resentment for the special treatment she received. Occasionally, her friends were invited to parties at the cottage. But they didn't visit daily.

Rosie plays miniature golf

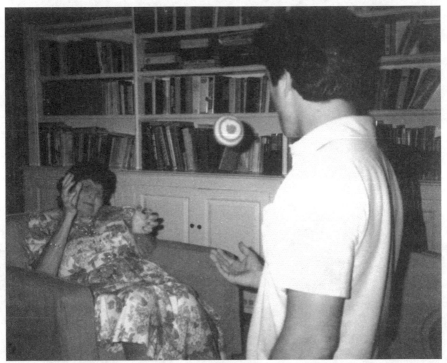

Rosie and Timothy Shriver play catch

They often danced, ate snacks, listened to music, or bowled together at the convent's one-lane alley. Like her mother, Rosie was an avid walker, and she'd head out on foot, year-round, weather permitting. She loved to socialize during her strolls, too.

"If it is a boy, watch out!" said Sister Paulus, laughing.

"Do you mean she likes to flirt?" I once asked my aunt.

"Why yes, I guess she does!"

"She doesn't stop to talk to the girls on her walks?" I asked.

"No," said Sister Paulus. "Just the boys."

"Does she have a boyfriend?" I asked my aunt.

Sister Paulus laughed. "No. She flirts with *all* of them!"

Above: Rosie decorates eggs for Easter
Below: Rosie smiles during the holiday festivities

One day my aunt took Rosie to my Uncle Arnold's house, and his daughter Joanne dropped by with her three young children. The attention quickly shifted from Rosie to Joanne's youngsters.

Rosie frowned and shouted, "She don't like them babies! She don't!"

Sister Paulus talked soothingly to her and gently held her hand. Rosie calmed down, but she was clearly perturbed not to be in the spotlight of center stage.

The more physically and mentally capable residents at Saint Coletta received life skills training to help prepare them to live in apartments or group homes. Some even had jobs. Unfortunately, Rosemary couldn't work; and besides, unlimited public access was not practical, for she *was* a Kennedy.

Because of her diminished capabilities, forging a life on her own while upholding the family's name, status, and exacting standards was out of the question. Joe Kennedy had made every effort to protect his eldest daughter, even if doing so meant containing her in a bubble. Rose had tried to free her, if just a little.

FAITH

"I need to operate immediately," the doctor said after examining older brother Leo, who was not yet twenty-two.

Dr. Notbohm surveyed the Koehler kitchen table. He ordered it to be scrubbed and then draped with a clean sheet. Large enough to seat all ten children and their parents, Kathryn and Harry, the table could accommodate Leo, who stood nearly six feet tall.

Arnold and Al quietly carried Leo from their upstairs' bedroom down the narrow wooden stairs to the kitchen. Leo moaned from pain as the brothers placed him on the table for surgery. Kathryn leaned over her son to press a cool hand on his fevered forehead. A nurse who assisted that day ushered Arnold and Al from the room and closed the door.

The family gathered in the parlor. Elmer, who at six years old was the youngest child, grabbed big sister Stella's hand for comfort. She squeezed it and whispered to him, "Elmer, we will pray for Leo. We will pray."

The wait began. The clock on the fireplace mantel slowly ticked the minutes away. Harry led Kathryn, his brothers Frank and Charlie, and his children in the rosary. They knelt in prayer, each with prayer beads in hand, eyes focused toward the crucifix hanging on the wall. When the kitchen door at last swung open, the physician shook his head.

"I'm afraid I have bad news," Dr. Notbohm said solemnly. "Infection has already set in. There is no hope. It is just a matter of time now."

A grief-stricken Kathryn cried aloud while the girls pulled out their handkerchiefs, and the boys paced the room. Although they had engaged in a prayerful death watch, there was no miracle for Leo in 1925, for penicillin had not yet been discovered.

When Arnold, who had been working at a factory nearby, heard the church bells toll a few days later, he knew his brother had passed away. As was the custom, Leo was laid out in the parlor where friends and relatives would come to pay their respects.

"My dear, we are so sorry," Aunt Tilly said to Kathryn, grasping her in a hug.

"Thank you," said Kathryn. "He is watching over us from heaven now as one of God's angels."

Twelve years later, in 1937, Anita died. She was just twenty-eight. The loss was especially difficult for Stella. Although Anita had died from tuberculosis, and thus less unexpectedly than Leo, the sisters had been close in age and personality. For the Koehlers, as it would be for the Kennedys, faith made it possible to move forward even in the midst of crushing sorrow.

TRAGEDY

In the early afternoon of November 22, 1963, President Kennedy's mother, Rose, was relaxing at their family's sprawling compound on Cape Cod, Massachusetts. Joe, having finished lunch with Rose, was napping. Rose decided to lie down, too, but a radio blasting from another room disturbed her rest. *Why does Ann have the television turned up so loud? The blare will wake up Joe.* Perturbed, Rose got up and joined Ann, her young niece. An announcer interrupted the regular program with a news bulletin: The president had been wounded in Dallas.

Concerned, Ann turned to Rose.

Rose comforted her. She said she was sure Jack would pull through. He had faced so many close health calls during his life, and he had survived every one. Rose stared through a window to the ocean beyond, remembering how Jack had nearly died from scarlet fever as a toddler. And then there was hepatitis, back surgery, and the terrible infection that followed. According to family legend: "If a mosquito bit Jack Kennedy, the mosquito would die." [40]

Ann, too, predicted that Jack would be all right, though she was more worried than she admitted.

They both thought of the World War II incident in 1943 when a Japanese destroyer had sunk Jack's PT-109 boat in the South Pacific. He had saved his crew, but the back injuries sustained during the rescue led to a life of chronic pain. He lived afterward with Addison's disease, digestive troubles, and numerous sports injuries. All caused him various amounts of discomfort, but he soldiered on. He even famously downplayed his wartime heroism with the quip: "It was involuntary. They sank my boat."[41]

Rose and Ann agreed not to tell Joe the news. They knew that the debilitating stroke that had rendered him speechless and wheelchair-bound two years before had also caused him to become highly emotional. They didn't want to alarm him unnecessarily.

Ann unplugged the radio before going up to her uncle's room. Rose unplugged the TV. When Joe awoke up from his nap, various friends and relatives casually wandered in and out of his room, chatting as though nothing unusual had happened.

<hr>

When I learned President John F. Kennedy had been assassinated, I, like many Americans, was stunned. Because my aunt took care of his sister Rosie, he was part of our family. As a six year old, I considered him to be my friend. He took care of our country and made sure we were all safe. *What will happen to us now? I wondered. Will the Soviet Union take over?*

The school bell rang and I ran outside, straight into my mother's arms. I shut my eyes tight, but tears still flowed down my cheeks.

"I'm sad, too, Elizabeth," my mother said. "He was a good man. But he's in heaven now."

She gently smoothed my hair until I relaxed.

As we walked the mile home together, I kicked the brown

and orange leaves with my feet. We passed the LaBelle Factory, a metal fabrication company in our hometown of Oconomowoc. The familiar, rhythmic clunks and thumps of its large machines had gone strangely silent.

I thought about Caroline Kennedy. Her birthday was in just a few days, as was mine. We were the same age. Poor Caroline. There would be nothing happy about her birthday without her father there. And I liked little John-John so much I had named my teddy bear after him. Would John-John understand he'd never see his daddy again?

My mother and I took our regular shortcut through the grassy field, a well-worn path behind the Quick Cleaners, where the smell of laundry chemicals blew hot air through vents and the back door. Workers stood near the back door, smoking, talking, and crying. It seemed as though the whole town had come to a stand-still.

I imagined my aunt hugging Rosemary, Sister Paulus' long black robe gathering around her, the stiff material against her skin.

"Will Rosemary be all right?" I said, looking up at my mother and sniffling as the sun moved behind a cloud.

"She might not understand about losing her brother," said Mom. "But she'll be sad because she can sense when the nuns feel bad. But you know Sister Paulus makes her feel happy, and they'll take her to the dorms next door so she can be with friends her age."

By the time I got home, my head was pounding. I lay down on the couch, and Mom draped a cool washcloth across my forehead. She sat with me, and when Dad came home from work at Fiberesin, a plastics manufacturing plant, the three of us hugged. There were tears in Mom's eyes. I had never seen her cry before.

Newsreel footage of Jack and Rosie before departing for England

Rosie and Jack in their youth

As the whole world waited for news, Rosemary, then forty-five and being cared for by the Sisters of Saint Francis of Assisi at Saint Coletta in Jefferson, Wisconsin, watched television along with the horrified nuns. The sisters prayed their rosaries and watched in silence.

Rosemary stared ahead.

When they quietly told Rosie about what had happened to her brother, she was sad but continued to watch the tragedy unfold on the television screen, according to the nuns assisting her.

Once news of the president's death reached all of his brothers and sisters, they gathered at the family home in Hyannis Port. Only one was missing—Rosemary.

❧❀❧

After Jack's death, his wife, Jackie, said, "The song he loved most came at the very end of this record, the last side of *Camelot*, sad *Camelot*, 'Don't let it be forgot, that once there was a spot, for one brief shining moment that was known as Camelot.'"[42]

For the next generation, Camelot symbolized the hopes and ideals of a nation as embodied by the Kennedys. The president's death left many to wonder: *What if he hadn't died?*

When Rose Kennedy learned of Jack's death, she left the house on foot for the beach, where her nephew, Joe Gargan, later joined her. "Joey, we must go on living," she said. "We can't look back." [43]

Rose kept her pain deep within herself; she coped by turning to prayer.

When Jack's youngest brother, Ted, arrived, he went upstairs to his parents' bedroom to break the news to Joe.

If Rose's stoicism was perceived as coldness by some, it also signaled her epic determination to endure and face the future with hope. Every family copes with tragedies in its own way. How it moves on in spite of loss helps determine its future.

My Misdiagnosis

The day I played kickball in our school's gymnasium, the winter of my freshman year in high school, turned out to be a turning point in my life.

I kicked the ball and it soared. At that very same moment, I ran full force into an unexpected opening door. *Slam!*

I woke up in a pool of blood. I thought stitches and a scar through my right eyebrow would be my only reminder of the incident. But later, when I managed to shift positions on the floor, all I saw was black, and the world swirled around me. My parents took me to my Milwaukee pediatrician, Dr. V., who ordered an electroencephalogram.

We were stunned by the diagnosis—epilepsy, a condition that, at that time, was never to be revealed because of the associated stigma. I knew of one student who suffered from seizures, and everyone at our school gave him wide berth.

I feared if my parents made known *my* diagnosis, I might be ostracized, too. I would be like Rosemary—someone whose family was ashamed, frightened, and upset. The Kennedy family kept Rosemary's diagnosis a secret, and now mine was doing the same.

Oconomowoc High School, which Elmer, Elizabeth's father, attended in 1934. For Elizabth, this building served as the site of her junior high and freshman year of high school.

Dr. V. prescribed pills for me. The spinning and blindness episodes got worse. Now they were accompanied by sickening headaches. I was forced to stay home from school, and I hated it.

The doctor increased my medication to reduce my symptoms. The headaches worsened. Not only that, but I felt like I was trapped in a fog. My ability to reason out my school homework slowed. And when I moved, dizziness overcame me.

When I discovered that my medical bills had forced my parents to take out a second mortgage on the house, I felt overwhelmed by guilt.

Why is this happening to us? Is it my fault? Is there anything I can do to stop it? Sometimes I tested myself. I'd stand up fast to see if doing so blinded me. I'd bend low or turn around, and the room would whirl.

Not only was the spinning out of my control, but so was my health. My parents were so concerned they took me to a hospital.

Elizabeth in junior high

"Do you have your medication with you?" asked Dr. V in my hospital room.

Mom handed it to him. He pocketed it and we never saw him, or my medical records, again. A new physician ordered more tests and indicated Dr. V's diagnosis was incorrect. It took a while for the medication's after-effects to wear off. Although I eventually improved, the symptoms didn't go away completely.

"Did my gym accident cause my health issues?" I asked.

"Possibly," said the new doctor.

As an adult, after a neurologist diagnosed me as having

migraines, he told me that low blood pressure can cause directional temporary blindness. I outgrew the blindness, but I never forgot the misdiagnosis or the doctor's cover-up.

Because the original diagnosis of epilepsy was clouded by shame, my parents and I kept my ordeal a secret, even from the rest of our family. Only my mother's older sister knew the truth. Later, I learned Rosemary had epilepsy. Her symptoms began as a young woman. She continued with anti-seizure medications while at St. Coletta. It apparently controlled her seizures, or at least my aunt never mentioned them.

There were cheerful moments during this difficult period. When I had a medical appointment, Mom and I rode the Greyhound bus from Oconomowoc to Milwaukee. We'd then take city buses to and from the doctor, and that could turn our office visit into an all-day affair in Milwaukee. We'd eat a home-packed bag lunch to save money, and if I wasn't too sick that day, Mom continued a childhood tradition for me: I'd get to buy a milk chocolate-covered pretzel wrapped in crinkly wax at the candy counter in Gimbel's Department Store.

I'd bite into the delicious combination of milk chocolate and salt and savor the satisfying crunch. With my parents' love and chocolate-pretzel moments, I got through the guilt, pain, and isolation my illness caused.

What was Rosemary's chocolate-pretzel moment? When she gazed out into the distance and seemingly laughed for no reason, I wondered if she was dancing with Jack in a ballroom, or dressing for her débutante's presentation. Perhaps she was swimming with her family at Taggart's Pier, or Eunice was steering their sled as they tobogganed.

Sister Paulus, Sister Julaine, and Rosie visited me at home during my illness. Rosie smiled and didn't seem to care that I wore my old bathrobe. To avoid dizziness, I moved as slowly as she did.

My aunt hugged me and handed me two gifts: a prayer book, which Mrs. Kennedy had inscribed with her best wishes for my good health, and a delicate, filigree, palm-sized silver tray, which I still display in my home.

At one point during my at-home recuperation, I said to Mom, "I really want to go for a walk." I was tired of being cooped up in the house.

"But what will people think if they see you outside?" asked Mom. "It will look like you're playing hooky. Maybe they'll think you're faking it and we're allowing you just to stay home for the fun of it."

She was right. I was hidden because of my illness.

Just like Rosemary.

During another recovery day at home, I looked at myself in a mirror. My thin legs, flat stomach, and slim body had vanished. Now I had flabby thighs and a tummy! I gasped.

"You're eating but not exercising," my mom said, holding a stack of laundry brought in from the outside line.

"I'll have to walk laps in the house," I said.

"And eat more salad," she suggested.

I was stunned to realize how quickly pounds could appear. When Rosie visited me, I noticed how slowly she lumbered along, and now I understood why she was hefty—not obese, but definitely not thin. Focusing on healthy eating had to be hard for those who cared for Rosie. How could anyone deny her the simple pleasures from her favorite part of the meal: dessert?

One day, a social worker came unannounced to our home. I felt as though I were a fraud, trying to put one over on the school system. When she left, I confessed my feelings to my mother. She felt the same way. I think that if we had told the social worker the truth about the health issues I was struggling with, our guilt would have vanished. But holding back information was second nature to my mother's secret-keeping generation. And she had a point: How much did they need to know? We weren't scamming anyone. I *was* sick.

When my mother was a child in the early 1930s, her mother was ill and Mom took care of her brothers and sisters. When a neighbor stopped by the house to "help," she ran a finger down the banister, checking for dust. Mom and her siblings worried. *Would the family be broken apart and sent to foster homes because of dust on the banister?*

I wondered about Rose Kennedy. What had she told people who came over and saw a young Rosie engaging in a tantrum? If she evaded the truth, did she feel guilt too?

❦

When I eventually returned to school, it was as though I were let out of prison. I could walk anywhere I chose! I joined the drama club, wrote for the school newspaper, and got a part-time job at the local library. Life was exhilarating, colors were vivid, food was delicious, and friends were more fun!

I've been fortunate that my childhood head injury didn't result in a serious impairment. However, I have suffered from severe headaches, which were later diagnosed as migraines, all my life. With dietary changes, exercise, and medication, I've learned how to cope with this chronic condition.

I had lost nearly a year of my teenage life due to illness. Although my temporary isolation paled in comparison to Rosie's, our shared experience cemented the bond between us.

Elizabeth returns to high school after her illness

After my diagnosis was corrected, I retained a sense of guilt over causing my family additional financial strain. Why didn't my parents ask the Kennedys for help? Because they were of proud stock. Midwesterners! Wisconsinites! It just wasn't in their moral fiber to ask for help; they only worked harder, and taught me to do the same. I knew this to be true of my relatives and friends' families as well. We were all raised to have a strong work ethic. *You can do it!* That was, and is, our motto. I'm very happy to come from such people who show no sense of entitlement.

My dad held three jobs. He worked at Fiberesin, a local plastic manufacturer, lined athletic fields for the city, and drove occasional paper routes. Dad was happy and never complained about long hours or the monotony of factory work. He came home from long work days smelling of fresh wood. To this day, I treasure that scent.

During high school and summers home from college, I held three jobs: I shelved and sorted books and created catalog cards for the public library, worked as a teacher's assistant for elementary summer school, and took orders and billed for Bonded Spirits, a local liquor sales and distribution company. Fortunately, I loved all three jobs.

My mom kept a full garden and made everything from scratch—from foods to curtains to clothing, and even the patterns for our clothing! She washed clothes with a wringer washing machine and carted all that wet laundry from our basement to our backyard, hanging them on clotheslines to dry.

Dad drove the family car, which he bought used, and shared it with me when I worked late hours. Mom and I walked or biked everywhere in town. I never went hungry, even during the lean times of the 1973 recession when Dad was laid off from his factory work. He and Mom saved their pennies and believed in paying off their credit card balances at the end of every month.

My dad's older brother Carl, Mary's father, worked hard on his farm and held down other day jobs while raising *fourteen children*. My cousins became hard workers and made contributions to society through volunteer efforts to various causes, and through church work.

One of Carl's daughters, Paula, not only works at a St. Coletta residential home and raises her four children, including one who is disabled, but she is also an active minister's wife and delivers newspapers on her bike in the early morning hours. The last time I visited her, she made several homemade pies to share with me and other relatives. Outside in her backyard, I noticed the day's freshly clean laundry flapping in the breeze.

I've nicknamed her Saint Paula.

EUNICE

Authors have written numerous accounts of Joe, Jack, Bobby, and Ted. But, for this story, the truly important Kennedy is Eunice.

In 1962, Eunice greeted her sister Rosie for the first time in twenty years.

1962 would prove to be a pivotal year for Eunice. Besides a reunion with a long lost sister, it would become the inaugural year for Camp Shriver, and on September 22nd, her essay "Hope for Retarded Children" was first published in *The Saturday Evening Post*. There seems no doubt that two decades of absence and thoughts of her missing sister had a profound effect on the direction of her life. Years before her reunion with Rosemary, Eunice had visited institutions, spoken with doctors and experts, and discovered how the mentally disabled were often treated.

Seeing Rosemary again must have been a very welcome event, although she had changed. She was a heavy, house-bound forty-three-year-old woman, formerly energetic and now lethargic—a common tendency of the intellectually challenged. But Eunice motivated Rosemary to action, and Rosie inspired Eunice, too.

Eunice sits with Rosie during a physical therapy session

Eunice and Rosie together on vacation

She convinced the Joseph P. Kennedy Jr. Foundation, which was founded by Joe Kennedy in 1946 to memorialize the Kennedys' oldest son Joseph (he died in combat in 1944), to focus its resources and efforts on helping the mentally disabled.

It was Eunice who influenced Jack to create the President's Panel on Retardation. Energetic and fearless, she was never shy about expressing her opinions.

In 1963, when she spoke to the female members of the President's Committee on the Employment of the Handicapped, Eunice said in no uncertain terms that its record was "frustrating and dismal."[44] The disabled ". . . have received virtually no attention from this committee . . . yet retardation is as much of a handicap as the loss of a leg, deafness, or an emotional disturbance."[45]

She was so bold, she even criticized her brother, Jack, when he was president. "You should put more fire into your speeches," she once told him.

"And you," replied Jack, "should put more of your speeches into the fire."[46]

Eunice and Rosie

Eunice and her children with Sister Paulus

Sister Paulus, Rosie, Eunice, and Rose Kennedy at Hyannis Port

Ted, Rosie, and Eunice

Rosie and Eunice in D.C.

ROSIE GETS LOST

One late Sunday morning in the fall of 1975, Eunice met Rosemary, Sister Paulus, and Sister Julaine at Chicago's Hilton Hotel. Although the nuns had already been to church with Rosie, Eunice hadn't. She proposed taking Rosie by herself.

Stunned, Sister Paulus paused a moment to reflect.

"Mother Superior has always insisted we accompany Rosemary everywhere," said Sister Paulus. One of Rosie's guides walked in front of her, leading the way, and another encouraged her progress from behind.

Eunice assured Sister Paulus that Rosie would be fine. With misgivings, Sister Paulus acquiesced. When it came to Rosemary, Eunice was the boss.

As they left, Eunice promised to have Rosie back by 2:30 p.m.

Sister Paulus prayed. Understanding how distracted Eunice could become and how prone Rosemary was to wander off, she knew she had a lot of praying to do.

I can see what probably happened then. The strains of the closing hymn of music finished at St. Peter's around noon Sunday, and Eunice escorted Rosie out of the church and into the vestibule.

People jostled about, talking to Eunice. Having noticed the priest heading her way, she probably thought about reminding him to speak more about the disabled in his sermons. She shook his hand and leaned in to make sure he heard her specific points. Scanning the announcements on the bulletin board, she turned back to Rosie, but where was she?

She was here just a moment ago. Eunice looked through the throng of people congregated in the atrium. No tall, dark head could be seen.

Eunice rushed through the crowd, glanced inside the empty church, and then pushed her way through the front door. At the top of the stairs, she had a clear view of everyone scattered below.

She yelled her sister's name. Had anyone seen her?

Unbeknownst to Eunice, Rosemary had kept right on walking with the crowd out the church's front door. When there was no one to walk next to, a colorful display in a picture window in downtown Chicago probably caught her interest, or a tooting car horn could have motivated her to walk on, or the sight of a juicy hamburger on the side of a bus might have prompted her to follow it.

The big city of Chicago lured Rosie with blaring boom boxes, shouting strangers, and even blasting exhaust fumes. But exploding sensory images didn't overwhelm her. Rosie took Ritalin, which helped keep her calm, and she'd been well-cared for these many years. Her sense of peace continued and she plodded on, enjoying the fascinating new world that contrasted starkly with Jefferson, Wisconsin, the small country town where she resided most of the year.

Frantic, Eunice ran into the street and waved down a cruising police car.

Within minutes, the family was notified that Rosemary was missing. The police implemented an intensive citywide hunt for her.

Hours passed.

Meanwhile, Sister Paulus and Sister Julaine waited at the Hilton Hotel. Sister Paulus checked her watch. Eunice was punctual. But at 2:30, no Eunice. No Rosemary. *Where were they?*

Sister Paulus called Eunice's room. No answer.

Finally, in walked Eunice with a policeman.

"Where's Rosie?" asked Sister Paulus, hurrying to them.

"I lost her," said Eunice.[47]

They divided up their search-and-rescue efforts. Eunice and the policeman walked one way, and the nuns the other.

"We walked five miles," wrote my aunt in a letter to me. "But no Rosemary."

Sister Paulus, the Shrivers, and the Kennedys were overcome with worry. Rosie had been lost to her family for many years, but when her mother and siblings rediscovered her, they included her once again and intended to do so forever.

Just as important, Rosemary had no skills to navigate the city alone. She couldn't communicate clearly. And because of her family's prominence and wealth, and Rosemary's naiveté, she could be an easy target for anyone seeking a ransom for her safe return.

Five hours after she disappeared, a policeman found Rosie window-gazing across from The Art Institute of Chicago on Michigan Avenue.

Her church outing with Eunice was the last time Rosie ventured out without a nun or two by her side.

Today, had Rosie been lost, the outcome might have been quite different. In 1975, news of the missing Kennedy wasn't reported by the press until *after* she was home safely.

Sex Ed and Silence

When I was growing up, it was a Catholic family tradition to make sure girls knew how important it was to be "good," which meant not sleeping with a boy before marriage. When Sister Paulus had been a girl, not only did she lack any knowledge about sex, but her mother hid her own pregnancies with large house dresses and aprons and didn't tell the children about the new child soon to join their family. Stella and her siblings realized there'd be a new baby in the family only after the doctor appeared and went into their parents' bedroom, closing the door after him.

One of my paternal uncles had to call the priest on his wedding night to convince his innocent and shocked bride that what he was proposing to do with her was permitted by the Catholic Church.

During Rosie's youth, there were "good girls" and "bad girls." Rosie wasn't a "good girl" because she was naïve about men. Some had taken advantage of her, according to what Sister Paulus whispered to Mom and me when she, Sister Julaine, and Rosie came to our house one day.

"She was sneaking out from the convent at night and going to taverns to meet men for love," she said.

Sister Julaine nodded. Rosie rocked in my mother's chair. *Does she know we're talking about her?* I wondered. She had a faraway look in her eyes. Did these men claim to love her? Even at my age, I had an idea why they'd take advantage of Rosie. She had been vivacious, beautiful, and more than willing, and she lacked the social skills to first ask for a declaration of love. These men were despicable.

My mother and I nodded knowingly. But as a naïve twelve-year-old, I wasn't really sure what Rosie was doing with those men she met at the tavern. I only *pretended* to understand.

Although Mom and I didn't discuss sexual intercourse, we talked about everything else, including what women could expect to happen with their bodies, why they should make use of birth control, and the importance of equality for women. Mom was a feminist before either of us knew what the word meant. As for the mechanics of intercourse, I learned the basics from reading a teen magazine—and what a relief it was not to have that conversation with my parents! Through my parents' respectful interactions with me and with each other, I formed my own moral code, with self-respect at its foundation.

Growing up as a Catholic girl, I was not only expected to be "good" when it came to sex, but also to obey my teachers, parents, and authority figures. Of course I had to memorize a slew of prayers: the *Our Father, The Apostles' Creed,* the *Act of Contrition,* the *Hail Mary,* and others. That was a cinch, but I had real problems with some of the pesky tenets of the Catholic Church.

Who said women couldn't be priests? Men!

How can a mortal man make all your sins vanish?

Why could my Lutheran friend never find her way to heaven? Was there a test to take after you died to prove your religion? Jesus wasn't even Catholic, so why would he care?

Mom agreed with me. Dad kept quiet. Sometimes I took his silence as agreement, but now I know he mostly wanted to keep out of our way. Wise man.

But he never loved me less. Dad was a "good" Catholic in every sense of the word. He volunteered to help the poor through the benevolent Catholic group, The Saint Vincent dePaul Society, raised funds for the intellectually challenged through The Knights of Columbus, and loved everyone, whatever their beliefs.

Elmer in his apron, volunteering

When he was in his eighties, I introduced him to a friend of mine. The two of them enjoyed talking about baseball. After my friend left, I told Dad the man was gay.

"Oh," said Dad with compassion, "the poor man."

Toward the end of his life, when Californians were voting whether to legalize gay marriage, I explained the ballot issue to him so he would know how to vote. I held his absentee ballot in my hands. Riddled with Parkinson's Disease, he couldn't fill in the bubbles for himself, so I would have to do it for him.

"Proposition 8 forbids same-sex couples from marrying," I said. I shared with him the example of a friend of mine who had been with his loving partner for twenty years—and, if Prop 8 passed, the two of them could not legalize their union. I blinked tears away as I expressed my concern.

I explained that many liberal Catholics disagreed with the legal ban on gay marriage and that many such Catholics, including me, were voting against Prop 8. But, to be fair, I also told him what Pope Benedict thought: A marriage should only be between a man and a woman.

How did my father vote on Proposition 8 that day? With the Pope, of course, and I was the one who dutifully marked the ballot for him, affirming the ban on gay marriage that was overturned by judicial decree several years later.

Sister Paulus and I avoided debating the various positions of the Church, much as my mother and I had avoided discussing sex. I didn't want my aunt to know how vehemently I disagreed with the Church on such issues, though I occasionally hinted at it.

I asked her if she thought women would someday become priests.

"Not in my lifetime," she said.

I can see why the church would oppose such a change: If women take on priestly roles and gender differences diminish, the traditional structure of family might deteriorate. But what elder males in the Catholic Church are slow to realize is that it is spirit, strength, and fortitude that create character, not gender.

Today, I wish I had more deeply probed my aunt's feelings and beliefs. I wonder what she really believed: if her views had any kinship with my own, and if we would have found a common ground on which to understand each other's opinions.

One conversation we had when I was in junior high school did show me how our beliefs differed, at least at that time. My mother announced that she and I had to cut our visit short with Sister Paulus and Rosie because a friend and I were going to a concert.

"Is your friend Catholic?" Sister Paulus asked me.

"No," I said.

Sister hugged me goodbye. "Well now, you'll work to change that, won't you?"

I laughed and was about to make a joke, but Mom's warning glance signaled me that this was no time for humor. My aunt had meant what she said.

I remember that, in the '60s, when Sister Paulus didn't approve of something, she would put her tongue to the roof of her mouth and say, "Tsk, tsk, tsk."

But as I grew older, I never heard her do that again. Like the world around her, she was evolving. But she was still a nun.

The comment about my non-Catholic friend was a defining moment for me. Although my love for Sister Paulus never faltered, I realized I was an outcast in the context of my father's family. I didn't belong here. And although Sister Paulus loved me unconditionally, I was sure my beliefs were not shared by other Koehlers. By nature outgoing and chatty, I had a hard time keeping my thoughts and feelings to myself. It took a toll.

Because Rosemary hid her underground escapades with men, I wonder if, emotionally, she was aware that her parents wouldn't approve. If Rose and Joe Kennedy asked what she was doing on her adventures, would she have answered them truthfully? If she kept the truth to herself, she would have experienced another burden.

THE KOEHLER BRAND OF
CLAUSTROPHOBIC CATHOLICISM

While nuns would have lectured naive Rosemary and her peers about proper moral behavior for girls, she may not have been able to decode their euphemisms. Her mother, being a refined, proper woman, probably wasn't totally clear, either.

Even in the 1960s and early 1970s, I wasn't sure what *fooling around* actually meant. But I wasn't the only female Koehler confused about being a "good" Catholic girl. My cousin Mary, the oldest of fourteen children, also struggled with this when she reached puberty in the sixth grade. The nuns told Mary and the other girls in her class not to touch themselves immodestly because doing so was a sin.

What does that mean? Mary wondered.

Too embarrassed to ask anyone face to face, she waited for the darkness and privacy of a confessional to ask the priest.

"Go ask your mother," he said.

At home, she found her mother straddling a row of vegetables in the garden, her pregnant belly nearly touching the cucumbers below her.

"Don't put your hand down there," Mary's mother replied,

pointing toward Mary's crotch to clarify.

"Why would anyone do *that*?" asked Mary

"Because it feels good," her mother (my aunt) said, tucking vegetables into her apron pockets.

Mary walked back into the farmhouse feeling guilty. She had squeezed her legs together and *that* felt good. *Squeezing like that must be a mortal sin!* she thought.

Mary knew that in the Catholic Church, mortal sins were the most grievous ones, for they brought "death to the soul." *If one has a mortal sin on one's soul, one cannot take communion.*

Mary stopped going to confession. She also stopped receiving communion. Her mother paced the floors. *What has my daughter done that is so bad she doesn't take communion?*

Mary holds a baby with her siblings

No matter what her mother said to her, Mary wouldn't say why she wouldn't accept the body of Christ. So my aunt took Mary to Saint Coletta to see a priest-psychologist. Although Mary didn't tell the priest what was going on, he told her parents she had picked up on her mother's feelings.

"I was actually a sponge between my mother and the rest of the children," Mary recalled. "I absorbed the uncomfortable stuff and protected them from it."

Her mother suffered from postpartum depression bouts after several of her births. At the time, there was little information about this type of depression or what having seven children in seven and one-half years could do to a woman's hormones and health. *As for fourteen children?* Such a large brood meant an endless cycle of feeding, diapering, bathing, and otherwise caring for children while also keeping house and tending to the farm.

After recovering from the hormonal imbalances caused by her many pregnancies, Mary's mother stabilized and her struggles with depression eased.

The priest-psychologist told Mary, "Don't worry about confession and communion. Go back and take communion again." He relieved her of the burden of guilt that had engulfed her, and she was once again a practicing Catholic in good standing.

Mary was twenty-three when her eighteen-year-old brother, Tom, drowned while playing with friends in a river. When the local pastor visited the family after receiving the tragic news, it proved to be a turning point for Mary. The priest was rigid and conservative. In his sermons, he harped on the evils of sex as a mortal sin. Her brother had died, and now this man stood before Mary's grief-stricken family. Her emotions boiled into anger.

She erupted inexplicably, yelling, "I don't like you!"

For a "good" Catholic girl, this seemingly minor action amounted to a radical moment of departure from the Church.

Mary had no one to turn to. "We weren't a family of shared feelings," she recalled.

She coined a term for our family and its foundation: "Claustrophobic Koehler Catholicism."

At about the same time, another Koehler cousin, Joanne, and her husband helped establish a liberal interfaith social justice group. It supported progressive ideas that included feminism, civil rights, and opposition to war. I was twenty years younger than Joanne, and given the silence surrounding me and the size of the Koehler brood, I typically saw my aunts, uncles, and cousins only rarely. For decades I didn't realize that we had shared similar philosophies.

In 1989, I wrote a letter to *Ms. Magazine,* recounting the disparity in my mother's wages relative to the pay her male counterparts received while working as bookkeepers in the 1940s. My cousin Mary read the letter and resumed our communication. I was no longer alone in the Koehler family.

Rosie's Three Families

Sister Paulus accompanied Rosie whenever she flew to Kennedy and Shriver homes in Hyannis Port, Massachusetts, where they slept in John F. Kennedy's childhood bedroom; Palm Beach, Florida; Chicago, Illinois; and Washington, D.C. Sister Paulus was quite the jet-setter when Midwesterners from small communities like ours considered air travel a big deal.

But getting Rosie to her destination often proved challenging. In an essay for our family called "Memories," my aunt wrote: "Traveling alone with Rosemary was not always easy, but our guardian angels were with us. While with the families, we were treated like one of them. God bless them." [48]

"Rosie, come along now," said Sister Paulus, leading the way.

Rosie plodded, shuffling her feet.

"Walk faster, Rosemary," said Sister Julaine, approaching from behind her.

"She don't *want* to!" shouted Rosie. "She don't."

Sister Paulus stopped in the middle of the airport and held Rosemary's hand. "Now Rosie, the quicker we get on the plane, the more fun we'll have looking out the window! Remember?"

Sister Paulus, Rosie, and Sister Julaine at Boston's Logan Airport

Rosie smiled. My aunt made sure Rosie stayed reasonably calm when she traveled. Managing Rosie and keeping her happy was like taking care of a toddler.

"Here's a restroom," said Sister Paulus. "Let's go now before we board."

Rosie's favorite part of every plane trip was the in-flight meal. Once she heard the familiar clink of silverware and trays and smelled food, her mood and face brightened and she sat up straight. She was always ready to eat!

The Kennedys and the Shrivers made sure Rosie felt welcome each time she visited. They knew her favorite form of entertainment—parties. So they threw her one nearly every time she came.

Rosie is entertained on a sunny outing

"Look, Rosie! Balloons! Streamers!" Sister Paulus pointed out the colorful decorations.

Rosie clapped her hands together and jiggled up, down, and sideways.

"And cake!" added Sister Paulus.

Rosie sat down and jabbered as if to say, "Let's get on with it!"

Rosemary's family loved music, and there was usually a piano nearby.

Eunice had noticed Rosie's reaction whenever Jean played "When Irish Eyes are Smiling" and Ted sang along. Rosie tapped her feet and swayed to the beat. Her eyes sparkled and her smile spread ear to ear. Rosie eventually became the proud owner of an electric upright player-piano.

Rosie at her player piano

There are no public records on whether Joe visited Rosie before his stroke. Because Joe often relied on his trusted friend, Eddie Moore, to look out for Rosie while she was in England and Joe was serving as the U.S. Ambassador, we might surmise that Eddie continued the practice back in the states.

After 1961, Rosie's mother and siblings—Jean, Pat, and Ted—occasionally visited her in Wisconsin. Her sister Eunice came the most often. And it seemed as though Rosie responded most warmly to her brother, Ted. As far as I can determine, Jack and Bobby never visited, nor did the wives, husbands, or children of Rosie's siblings, except for Anthony Shriver, Eunice's fourth son.

He began regular trips to Rosie in the 1980s, forming a bond with his aunt and discovering his true calling: serving the intellectually challenged. In 1989, he founded Best Buddies International, a global nonprofit organization that fosters one-to-one friendships between people with and without intellectual disabilities.

He remembers his aunt fondly. "She was an avid swimmer, and had this extraordinary capacity to swim for what seemed like hours ... She had such physical stamina and resilience." [49]

Anthony Shriver with Rosie and his daughters

Not only was Rosie reclaimed by her own family midway in her life, but she had truly become part of the Saint Coletta family. In a sense, she was also a member of our family. One fall day in the early 1970s, after a busy summer during which my parents and I weren't able to see Sister Paulus and Rosie, we headed to Saint Coletta for a visit. I had grown taller and Rosie noticed.

"You no Baby Jack no more!" she said, stomping her foot when I walked in the front door.

Why had she called me by her brother John's nickname? Maybe her fondness for me was her way of transferring the love she had felt for her brother. Maybe she considered me a small part of her family and life.

"Rosie, I'm sorry," I said to her.

"No!" She refused to look at me. "You no Baby Jack no more!"

"Now Rosie," said Sister Paulus. "You love Elizabeth! Even though she is taller, she is still Elizabeth."

"You no Baby Jack no more," she mumbled.

By the time of my next visit, Rosie had forgiven me, or perhaps my aunt had convinced her I wasn't to blame for growing taller—and *older*.

Somehow, Rosie made a connection between her brother Jack and me. He was a year older than her, but Rosie could have grown taller than him at an earlier age. Jack was a sickly, thin child and she was healthy and robust. The lobotomy hadn't erased her memory completely, and it's possible she remembered Jack as a young child.

From left: The author, her father, Sister Paulus, and Rosie at Sister Paulus' 50ᵗʰ Jubilee

Rosie owned a miniature gray poodle named Lolly. She was an affectionate and friendly dog, but Rosie didn't cuddle or pet her without encouragement. Still, Lolly was a lively addition to Rosie's household and, as a dog lover, I had great fun with Lolly. Once when greeting me, Lolly jumped into my lap and licked my face.

"Don't let her do that," said Sister Julaine.

"Oh, it's all right," said my mother. "We're used to Elizabeth by now. She lets every dog she meets kiss her that way."

"She might give Lolly germs," said Sister Julaine, sounding perfectly serious.

Sisters Charles, Paulus, and Julaine with Rosie and Lolly

Most people didn't recognize Rosemary on the street. However, the staff at Saint Coletta was very protective of her. If an unfamiliar person or car passed by Rosie's home, a nun or aide would question the stranger in a friendly manner. More than once while we were visiting there, a vehicle slowly passed by Rosie's house.

"I'll take care of him," said my dad one time.

He paused at the driver's lowered window and asked if the stranger needed directions. The passerby turned out to be a polite gawker who had heard President John F. Kennedy's sister lived at Saint Coletta and had driven by hoping for a glimpse of her.

Sister Paulus, Anthony Shriver, Rosie, and Eunice

Rosie had a profound influence on us; she made us all better people. Her sweet, gentle nature bloomed during her relationship with my aunt. Her innocence and childlike, loving behavior made us feel great compassion. It made us ask ourselves, "If Rosie, overwhelmed by an unfortunate tragedy, can act with love, grace, and respect, what can I do? What *should* I do?" She made us want to be our better selves and inspired us to donate what time and energy we had to those less fortunate.

From a young age, my mother regularly took me to visit people at Shorehaven, a local nursing home for the elderly. When I was in second grade, my mother showed me and a friend how to make panorama Easter eggs; delicate, hollow, sugar eggs with a tiny diorama inside. It seemed a symbol of what Rosie had become. And, if we looked closely enough, we discovered what inner beauty and strength she gave us.

After creating trays of these sparkling delicacies we delivered them to Shorehaven. It was there I befriended one of the residents, a woman I'd call "Grandma."

When I was in junior high, someone at Shorehaven asked me to write letters for a blind woman who lived there. I did this for years.

Despite limited financial means, my parents wanted to do as much as they could for the church, so they asked me to play the church organ in hopes of satisfying what they considered our "debt." Looking back on all this, I feel sorry for the churchgoers forced to suffer through my probably mangled renditions of Catholic hymns. Meantime, my dad ushered for the church, served as treasurer of St. Vincent DePaul, and regularly visited sick and elderly parishioners.

My Koehler relatives also had this volunteering spirit, and expressed it with their own civic and church communities. They continue to be active today.

One day when Sister Paulus, Rosie, and Sister Julaine appeared at my family's front door, all three were bouncing with excitement. Even my dog, Laurie, wiggled and barked, picking up on their enthusiasm.

Sister Julaine and Rosie entered the house first, with Rosie grinning and hopping. Although she typically walked slowly and a bit hunched over, she seemed to be standing straighter, and she was so excited we thought she was going to leap up and down.

"Yip! Yip!" Laurie rolled over on her back and kicked her paws in the air.

"What's going on?" asked my mother.

Rosie, Sister Paulus, Aunt Ruby, and Sister Julaine

Sister Julaine looked behind her, waiting for Sister Paulus to appear.

The screen door opened. Sister Paulus asked, "Did you tell them?"

"No," said Sister Julaine. "I thought you should."

"Somebody better," I said. "I can't stand the suspense anymore!"

"Rosie read billboards!" said Sister Paulus.

Mom, Dad, and I gasped.

Rosie seemed a foot taller and was clearly bursting with pride.

No one moved for a whole minute. Rosie giggled!

For no apparent reason—and for the first time ever—Rosie had read aloud all the large signs lining Highway 16 as she and the nuns drove from Jefferson to Oconomowoc, which was more than twenty miles.

We treated Rosie like a queen that day.

"Rosie, you get to be served first!" said my mother.

Rosie beamed.

"Congratulations, Rosie!" I said, hugging her. "I am so proud of you!"

After we toasted Rosie with lemonade and Mom's homemade date cake, Sister Paulus opened her purse and pulled out Rosie's greeting cards. Rosie reached for them gratefully, as a child might for a favorite toy. She glowed as she shuffled the cards, then paused to study the picture on each one.

The billboard experience motivated my aunt to use flashcards with Rosemary, and she was successful in teaching her to read simple words in children's books.

Commenting on Rosie's accomplishment, Dr. Steven Holtz, a neurologist at the University of California, Berkeley, said a prefrontal lobotomy doesn't damage the area of the brain involved in reading and spoken language. Rosemary's doctors could have damaged but not eliminated her ability to read, he said. "One assumes she could probably understand and follow directions." [50]

On a lunchtime visit to Saint Clare Cottage, my parents and I, along with the three sisters and Rosie, sat comfortably at the large table in the spacious dining area. From the picture window we could see maple trees exploding in brilliant oranges and reds. Outside, young men and women walking to and from Alverno waved to us as they passed by. We waved back.

My aunt, Sister Charles, and Sister Julaine refused our offers to help with the meal preparation. We were the guests and they wanted to serve us. After we all sat down and said grace, we passed meatloaf, potatoes, green beans, and gravy around the table.

"May I have the butter?" asked my mother.

Rosie looked at the butter in front of her plate. She reached down and handed it to my mother.

"Thank you," said Mom.

For a moment, there was complete silence.

Then the nuns called out with excitement.

"She did it!" said Sister Julaine.

"She passed the butter!" said my aunt.

"She's never done *that* before," said Sister Mary Charles.

"I wonder why," said my aunt.

"Good job, Rosie," I said.

Rosie beamed.

I wondered: *What exactly are Rosie's limits? What are her untapped possibilities?* The label "retarded" had stuck with her so long that everyone assumed she lacked even basic abilities. *If the expectations had been higher for Rosie, might she have risen to them? What if . . .*

Mom and I asked Sister Paulus if Rosemary really had been mentally retarded before her lobotomy.

"No. She was learning disabled," said my aunt.

"An individual who could do complex mathematical problems

is unlikely to be retarded," said Dr. Steven Holtz, a neurologist on the faculty of University of California, Berkeley. "Often, learning disabilities will be associated with a misperception that an individual is retarded or intellectually abnormal."[51]

"Agitated depression is psychotic depression," Dr. Holtz added, "which means she was delusional. It's not uncommon for the onset (psychotic depression) to occur during the age range of 18–25."[52]

I felt sorry for Rosie. For the most part, she was unable to read, write, or communicate clearly. But I saw how she thrived when she was treated with gentleness and afforded freedom, even just a little freedom. Indeed, I witnessed how she experienced and inspired joy in life more so than many able-minded people.

When I talked with Eunice's youngest son, Bobby Shriver, he said it best. "What an enormous blessing she was. If she hadn't lived, where would all of their [the Kennedys'] sensibilities have been? Who would have looked out for them [the intellectually challenged]? The whole tradition might have not materialized."[53]

※◇※

Though Eunice was the driving force behind the latter half of Rosie's life with the Kennedys, Ted Kennedy and Jean Kennedy Smith also visited and spent time with their sister. The following pages show just some of the occasions they enjoyed as a family.

Ted Kennedy, Rosie, and her St. Coletta family

Sister Charles, Ted, Sister Paulus, and Rosie

Rosie and Ted dancing

Rosie snaps a picture of Ted at dinner

Mrs. Kennedy, Rosie, Ted, and Sister Paulus at Hyannis Port

Sister Paulus and Rosie at Hyannis Port

Rosie poses on the stairs, Hyannis Port

Rosie and Sister Paulus visit Ted's house

Rosie and Ted

Ted Kennedy and Rosie enjoy a sunny lunch date

Rosie receives a gift from Jean

Rosie and Jean on family vacation

STANDING OUT

As my husband and I researched this book at the JFK Presidential Library in Boston, I read through documents at one table and Bob photographed various papers at another. Later, we stopped for lunch at the café downstairs.

"Mrs. Kennedy bought Rosemary a mink coat while she was living at Saint Coletta's," Bob said, shaking his head.

"Yes," I said. "She had no idea what Rosie needed or would have liked."

I flashed back to the image of my mother borrowing a mink coat for the photograph taken of her before marrying my father. Rosie's wearing that flashy coat among her friends and the plain rural people who worked at Saint Coletta was comparable to my mother sporting a mink while gathering eggs from the family's hen house.

What was Rose Kennedy thinking? As it turns out, she had gifted each of her daughters a mink coat. She treated Rosemary equally. Winters were cold in Wisconsin, just as they were in Massachusetts. Although the gift was expensive and would make Rosie stand out in her small community, it had a practical use, too—

it would keep her warm.

I suspect Rosie wore it when she visited her mother. Around us, she wore a comfortable, practical "Midwestern" cloth coat that fit in with everyone else's outer garments. Perched on her thick brown, curly hair was a colorfully knitted hat created by the nuns. On her hands she wore matching mittens.

As a child, my aunt had prayed on her knees hoping to trap a mink. The fifteen dollars the pelt would bring would go a long way on the family farm in the 1920s. I myself never wanted a mink coat. My most memorable article of clothing was my first communion dress. For a young Catholic girl in the 1960s, a first communion dress was as significant as the gown for a débutante ball. Family members attend the church service celebrating first communion, then gather for an at-home supper complete with a decorated cake.

Elizabeth at her First Communion, 1965

Elizabeth in line for her First Communion

In that era, many Catholic girls looked forward to making their first communion as eagerly as they anticipate their wedding day. I couldn't wait. The previous year, I had watched the other girls on their first communion day. They walked, two by two, from the hallway of Saint Jerome's school, out the door and up the church steps. Their frilly white dresses flounced and swished; even the rustling sounded fancy.

That night in my bedroom, I pretended I was twirling around in my communion dress, my arms outstretched, displaying layers of satiny petticoats for all the world to see. But when the time came for my first communion, my parents couldn't afford a "foo-foo" dress. Mom bought delicate eyelet material on sale and devised her own pattern to create a dress with a classic look.

I eyed the swatch of fabric. "No, Mom, no!" I cried, tears pouring down my face. "You can't make me a dress out of *that!*"

"E-liz-a-beth," she said, exasperated. "This is lovely." She fingered the cloth with a faraway look in her eyes. "What I wouldn't have given for a dress like this."

"Then *you* wear it," I said, running to my bedroom and slamming the door.

Throwing myself onto my bed, I sobbed and wondered why I was the only child in my class with such a cruel mother.

At the time of my holy communion, I was in second grade and knew I'd be the *only* girl wearing a non-frilly dress, which I was. Every other girl was ensconced in shiny, fancy-schmancy puffs of satin, sheen, and lace.

I was mortified.

The good girl in me froze in place. I stood up straight, but I felt like a troll doll in a long line of Barbie dolls. In that sea of frills, my mother stood tall with me.

All these years later, looking at the photo taken of me in the dress I wore that day, I'd love to have one *exactly* like it, too. Mom had good taste.

Mom made herself look good creating her own wardrobe from plain fabric, but she was always broke.

"Your mom had class," Aunt Dorothy said after Mom passed away. "The rest of us would look like something from the five-and-dime, but she was always stylish."

A mink coat and a communion dress—two mothers, each providing the best she could. Two daughters standing apart from their peers, sharing that sense of separateness, but as different as we could be.

In 1965, when I was seven years old, *The Sound of Music* played at a local summer stock theater in Milwaukee. My parents had saved up and bought three tickets. When the main character, governess and postulant Maria, shed her nun's habit and appeared on stage in a wedding gown for her marriage to Captain von Trapp, I shrieked.

The theatergoers turned their attention from the main stage to me.

"No!" I screamed, sobbing hysterically. My mother hugged me, both consoling me and attempting to muffle my loud cries in her embrace.

"What's the matter, Elizabeth?" she whispered.

"She's not *supposed* to get married!" I cried. "She's supposed to become a *nun!*"

On some level, I suspect I was afraid Sister Paulus would get married and leave the convent. I had a special relationship with her—one that was different from the relationships I'd formed with my other aunts. There weren't words to do justice to the bond we shared. Special? Spiritual? Deeply connected? None come close. At the time, I felt that if Sister Paulus were to stop being a nun, she'd become . . . well, *ordinary*. And I'd lose the special relationship I had with her.

Sister Paulus had the gift of making you feel as if you were the only one in the world who mattered. *You* were important. *You* were the best. She gave selfless, unconditional love. She must have made Rosie feel that way, too.

Although there is no mandatory age for retirement among nuns, Sister Paulus retired as Rosie's full-time caregiver in June 1983, at the age of seventy-three. Rosie was then sixty-four. Sister Paulus moved into a group home at Saint Coletta, where she supervised residents who cleaned the chapel. She continued to drive for the other nuns and residents, including Rosie, so she still saw her every week and traveled with her on out-of-town trips to the Kennedys and Shrivers.

"I do miss living with her all the time," she said to me one day after moving out of Saint Clare Cottage.

"Why did you decide to leave?" I asked her.

"At my age, I needed lighter responsibilities," she said.

One day, after she'd retired, my aunt and Sister Julaine stopped at Rosie's home for a visit. Another nun was helping Rosie in the bathroom.

"Hello!" called Sister Paulus as the screen door squeaked shut behind them. "Anyone home?"

Rosie jumped up, shouting and waving with her good arm.

"Umph ooh, tumble oy she!"

"Sit down, Rosemary," said the nun tending to her. "Finish what you're doing first before you greet Sister Paulus."

After Rosie had washed and dried her hands, she yanked the door open and hurried out to the living room. The sisters laughed as Rosie hopped up and down, embracing Sister Paulus and talking in her private language. It was like the reunion of two long-lost sisters.

In one of my last photographs of my aunt, she and Rosie are holding hands and beaming with delight. Rosie's smile at the camera seems to say: "Look at my best friend! We're together again!"

The years my aunt had spent with Rosie were the most rewarding of her entire career. She said it was her favorite time, because she was able to pursue her passion. I think she never realized how good she was when working with people with special needs. But it was during those times that Sister Paulus blossomed, as did Rosie. I think that was why it was such a joy to be around the two of them. Love and happiness emanated from both of them! Rosie's big smile was a gift I always felt, as was her rapid-fire talking to me. It said she was comfortable sharing her thoughts with me.

Rosie and Sister Paulus visit Washington, D.C. in autumn

Rosie and Sister Paulus just before Christmas

Sister Paulus, Rosie, and Sister Julaine visit the JFK Presidential Library

Sister Paulus and Rosie enjoy an album of postcards from their travels together

While doing research at the John F. Kennedy Presidential Library, I felt a rush of love when I found letters from Sister Paulus to Mrs. Kennedy. Even though they only dealt with pragmatic matters such as where they shopped for Rosie's clothes, or how much had been spent on a pair of shoes for her, I could picture my aunt carefully typing such letters and meticulously sealing them. That she *typed* them shows how much she respected Mrs. Kennedy.

My aunt, busy taking care of Rosie's emotional and physical needs, had numerous tasks to handle. She spent extra time with Rosie, teaching her life skills, helping her read with flashcards, swimming with her in the pool, taking her to socialize with other residents, and walking with her to make sure she exercised. She also took loving care of the vegetable garden and the many roses surrounding Rosie's house. She was a wonderful cook and baker, and canned many vegetables and fruits. In fact, she was well known for her fabulous strawberry jam. She loved driving, and chauffeured Rosie and the nuns to various appointments. I know she spent a great amount of time praying and, occasionally when we'd stop by for an unannounced visit, we'd find her in St. Coletta's chapel saying her rosary, or lighting candles for special intentions. My parents and I never understood how she kept everything running so smoothly. Though she had another nun helping her, she was always Rosie's favorite. So when Rosie didn't like something, it fell to Sister Paulus to use her gentle, almost magical abilities on her.

Where did she find the energy? My aunt was older than my dad by nearly ten years. I think that when you love your career and the people you work with, that passion gives you energy. Rosie gave as much as she received. As Anthony Shriver told me, it was a blessing she was here for us to find the best in ourselves.

In 1990, Anthony wrote to Sister Paulus: "If anyone has helped Rosemary in life, it is you! You have been the rose in her life."

In one letter my aunt wrote me after she retired, she said, "Rosemary spent Thanksgiving in New York with her sister Jean Smith. I drove them to the airport on Tuesday and called for them on Monday. "

In a few letters Sister Paulus wrote to me, she mentioned such things as taking Rosie to the doctor, or that they were leaving for a trip to visit Mrs. Kennedy, or taking Rosie to a restaurant after shopping. Living with Rosie daily was ordinary, even though she was from an extraordinary family.

I did long for letters or diary entries from my aunt which would express her true feelings. Alas, our family didn't raise people to share feelings that way or to write of intimate details. My aunt's diaries, and those of my father, were tiny palm-sized books where they recorded the weather, if the farm crops were thriving, and who helped with the threshing.

Searching for some hint of emotion, I looked at the dates when Leo became ill and died. Dad wrote: "Leo sick," for one date. "Doctor came," for another, and the last, "Leo died."

There was no time to feel sorry for oneself, let alone record it on paper. After all, cows had to be milked, grain planted, and a whole lot of other farm and house work done. Surviving was a full-time job.

I have a deep respect for the pragmatism of a farmer's writing, but I was delighted when I found an old Christmas card from Rosie.

When Sister Paulus or another nun would send mail from Rosie, she would write Rosie's name for her. Over her name, Rosie would then use her pen or pencil to make vertical lines, which was her way of signing.

Rosie sent us Christmas, thank-you, and thinking-of-you cards. We sent her cards, too, and gave her candy at Christmas.

After Sister Paulus passed away, my mother faithfully carried on the candy tradition, as did I. We both hoped Rosie and the hard-working nuns would enjoy the treats together.

A Christmas card signed by Sister Paulus and Rosie

During the course of writing this book, I took a break to visit a friend I hadn't seen since high school. When I told her about the stories behind this project, her jaw dropped.

"Your aunt took care of *Rosemary Kennedy*?"

I nodded.

"I never knew that!"

Why didn't she?

We visited Rosie nearly every month, but it wasn't a big deal for us. She was part of our everyday life. And there was an unspoken agreement among our family to keep not only our own secrets, but those we were trusted with. Rosie was part of a wealthy family. Although I don't believe telling my friends would have endangered her, it didn't seem right or fair at the time to broadcast the information.

While working on another writing assignment during this book's publication process, I interviewed a man in Wisconsin. When he asked about my upcoming book, I clarified who Rosemary was.

"You don't have to tell *me* who she is," he said.

"Many people don't know," I told him.

He replied, "The state of Wisconsin *owns* Rosemary Kennedy!" Of course I think he meant that with *love*.

Another Wisconsin native told me, "She was *our* Kennedy."

It might seem curious that Wisconsin *claims* Rosie, but there's good cause: Rosie came from a popular and powerful family, but she stood apart because of her vulnerability. I believe the best of people is revealed through adversity, and Wisconsin adopted her when she needed support. She became beloved.

Rosie was sweet, childlike, and innocent, and the compassion of the people of Wisconsin was reflected through the care and respect they showed her throughout St. Coletta, Jefferson, and beyond. These people have shown themselves to be well-grounded, with a strong sense of family. And, in an intangible way, they enveloped Rosie in their collective hearts.

❧❦❧

Today in my office, Rosemary's rosary, each bead a silver rose, adorns a crucifix. Below it I display the black and silver crucifix Sister Paulus wore. On my fireplace mantel is the delicate filigree tray given me by the Kennedys. I'm sure this, along with a few books signed by Mrs. Kennedy and Eunice, were really gifts from Sister Paulus to me.

Rosie receives a rosary, with Sister Julaine (left), Rose Kennedy, and Sister Paulus

Rosie holds up her rosary for the camera

Other than Mrs. Kennedy's kind invitation for me to visit Hyannis Port, there was no cause for greater interaction. When they planned their trips to see Rosie, Sister Paulus let us know so we wouldn't disturb their privacy. But in the 1980s, when my parents visited, Anthony was there too, and they lunched with him. By that time I lived in California, and my Wisconsin trips never coincided with his. My only interactions with the Shrivers were for this book.

The older Rose Kennedy was never able to establish a good relationship with the adult Rosemary. What a shock it must have been for Mrs. Kennedy to have experienced two such different personalities in one daughter. After being absent for twenty years of her daughter's life, during which Rosie changed physically and psychologically, how could she repair the damage and rebuild rapport with her?

She had to face tragedy each time she saw her daughter. Sister Paulus told me that Rose would sometimes gaze at her daughter, sigh, and say, "Rosemary, what have we *done* to you?"

Rosie never again displayed anger toward her mother after their traumatic (and dramatic) reunion at the Milwaukee airport, but she wasn't warm toward her mother, either.

"I see by her file she's gained three pounds," Mrs. Kennedy said to my aunt during one visit. "Is she still walking and swimming each day?" Rose Kennedy kept track of Rosemary much as she had her children when they were young, using note cards to detail their vaccinations, illnesses, and activities.

Stoic that she was, Rose Kennedy didn't share her suffering or her emotions. Rita Dallas, who was Joe's nurse, said after the president was assassinated, "She never complained or openly grieved, but night after night she could be heard pacing back and forth in her room." [54]

So when people say she was cold, it was a façade she presented to the world. She kept her heart inside, tightly wrapped. I'm convinced she loved her adult daughter very much but didn't know how to relate to her once Rosie became a different person than the one she had known as a child, adolescent, and young adult.

Rose Kennedy's forte was managing her bustling household and engaging in social and political conversation with diplomats, officials, and their spouses. How could she communicate with a daughter who couldn't converse as most people do? If only she had discovered what my aunt knew: Through the power of gentleness, praise, and love, an attachment can develop and grow stronger.

"I remember Grandma being a little more distant with Rosemary," Bobby Shriver told me. "Less if Teddy or Jean came [along]. Grandma would focus on them in a different way." [55]

In her memoir, *Times to Remember*, Mrs. Kennedy made it sound as though she and Joe had made the decision together to have Rosemary undergo a "certain form of neurosurgery." [56] She didn't mention being left out of the decision or not knowing about her daughter's whereabouts for two decades. She airbrushed the story of her life rather than detail the reality, which included dark, difficult times. Who could blame her?

Rose Kennedy with Sister Paulus

THE SPECIAL OLYMPICS

In 1962, when Eunice realized that children with special needs couldn't experience the fun of summer camp, she started Camp Shriver on the family's farm in Timberlawn, Maryland. Students volunteered as assistants and family members pitched in doing "grunt work," according to Bobby Shriver, the eldest son of Eunice and Sarge Shriver.

"I was seven," Bobby Shriver said, recalling the start of Camp Shriver, which later became The Special Olympics. "There were one hundred people in the house and on the two hundred-plus acres. I tried to help. They sent me off to get drinks for everyone. I'd get into the swimming race. It was wild and fun!" [57]

As a child, he recalled, camp days were exciting, with many teenagers around and activities happening everywhere on the family premises. "Special people were eccentric . . . There were colorful personalities among the campers." [58]

Eunice Kennedy Shriver in front of a tree with children in a circle at Camp Shriver

Each summer until 1968, Camp Shriver offered swimming, horseback riding, tennis, obstacle courses, rope climbing, running races, and arts and craft activities. One exercise involved kids jumping in and out of old automobile tires. And that was long before recycling was popular.

Eunice didn't just come up with the camp idea and let others do all the work. She was personally involved with the kids during the entire camping experience.

Recalling his wife Eunice's involvement, Sargent Shriver said: "When I'd come home from the office, there's my wife in the pool, holding this mentally retarded child in the water to see if it's possible for that child to swim. She didn't hire somebody for that. She went into that . . . pool herself. She's a hands-on person." [59]

Eunice saw the word "special" in a quotation on a wall at Saint

Coletta's. It "described retarded children as special to God. So I said that 'special' be used in front of the word Olympics." [60]

In July 1968, the first International Special Olympics was held at Chicago's Soldier Field. One thousand disabled people from twenty-six states and Canada participated in track-and-field and swimming competitions.

The event was a bright beacon in dark times. The country had been splintered by the Vietnam War. The Democratic National Convention burst into violence in Chicago only a month after the games. A mere seven weeks before, Eunice's brother Robert had been assassinated. Eunice, with the intrepid spirit that defined the Kennedys, kept her focus. These kids were counting on her. She moved forward with them.

Eunice Kennedy Shriver looking out at the 1968 Special Olympic Games

"Nobody is turned away," Eunice told Bob Addie, a *Washington Post* sportswriter about the Special Olympics. "Every child gets a chance to compete."[61]

Not only was it an outstanding experience for these kids to compete in the standing broad jump, the softball throw, the 300-yard run, or the 100-yard swim, but most of the participants had never been away from home before. This was their first banquet.

Mayor Richard Daley knew the 1968 Special Olympics marked a huge cultural change that would extend far beyond Chicago. Those once invisible were competing in athletics, socializing, and interrelating in ways never before imaginable.

"You know, Eunice," he said at the time, "the world will never be the same after this."[62]

Although some Saint Coletta residents participated in the Special Olympics, quiet and reserved Rosemary never did. Her family preferred to keep her out of the limelight.

Although Camp Shriver led to the Special Olympics, Camp Shriver sports camps exist today at sites located in Florida, Oregon, Louisiana, Missouri, and Massachusetts. Combining intellectually disabled campers with the non-disabled, the camps foster social inclusion as well as strengthen motor skills. And perhaps most importantly, everyone has fun!

Eunice had fun growing up as an athletic Kennedy—playing touch football on the lawn with her brothers and sisters, as well as competing in sailing races, tennis matches, and swim meets. It also empowered her. Her degree in sociology from Stanford and work in the juvenile court system helped prepare her to assist others with significant problems she had never experienced. Fundraising for her family's foundation laid the groundwork for the contributions she would make to support the intellectually challenged around the globe. While criss-crossing the world on behalf of the cause she championed, Eunice raised four children with her husband, and took charge of Rosemary's care when their mother's health faltered.

But perhaps it was her parents' influence that motivated her calling: their insistence on success, their offering of travel, academic, and cultural opportunities, and their insistence on giving the best of everything to their children. It created the finest star of all—Eunice.

Said Anthony Shriver, "My mother was the driver of Rosemary's life." [63]

By interacting as she did with Rosemary, she showed her children how to treat people. In this world of inequalities, it isn't a skill often shared.

"We judge a book by its cover. We fail to look at the spirit," said Timothy Shriver. "Throughout my life, Rosemary was a regular visitor, just like any other family member, although Rosie would stay longer and spend more time with me than most other family members." [64] Timothy Shriver is now Chairman of Special Olympics.

Rosie remembered. She eagerly anticipated reunions with her family, which included walks on the beach and swimming in the family pool.

A Kennedy Family Reunion

John Jr., Rosie, and Carolyn Bessette Kennedy

Rosie and Eunice

Rosie with the Shriver kids
Back: Mark, Bobby, Tim, Maria
Front: Rosie and Anthony

Anthony Shriver, his wife Alina, and Rosie

"I remember Rosemary coming when we'd drive from Boston to Hyannis Port," Bobby Shriver recalled. "She'd get all excited!" [65]

Eunice often joined her for those visits, and when she couldn't, she would chat with Rosie on the phone.

Anthony Shriver said, "She'd tell [Rosemary] all about her day and ask, 'Are you swimming? Not eating too much?' Then I'd get on [the phone] and tell her about my school. She [Eunice] would tell her about Uncle Teddy and what he had done. She'd send her [Rosemary] clippings about our family." [66]

Although Rosemary didn't respond verbally during these phone conversations, Eunice continued them, knowing Rosie was happy to listen to her sister.

Eunice was a tough taskmaster with the nuns as well as with Rosemary. "She'd tell the nuns that Rosemary had to get the weight off. 'No more cookies. I don't want her walking ten minutes. I want her walking a half hour,'" said Anthony. "She was hard on her [Rosie] because she wanted the best care she could get." [67]

"She treated Rosemary just like she treated Pat, Teddy, or Jean," said son Mark Shriver about his mother. "Mummy wasn't doing this out of pity. She [Rosemary] was a full-fledged human being. Rosemary would sneak sugar cookies. She would yell at Mother. 'Stop bothering me! Eunice, leave me alone!'" [68]

From his observations, Bobby Shriver thought my aunt was firm with Rosie when necessary, but also loving. "Sister Paulus was a very knowing person," he said. "She would talk to [Rosie] in a frank way more than the rest of us. Rosie would have little tricks if she didn't want to go to sleep or she wanted more food. Sister Paulus would say, 'No, you can't do this now.' I might say 'Why not?' But she'd be like a parent." [69]

Bobby Shriver laughed. "I saw how Rosie interacted with her," he said. "Sister Paulus was 'the man,' so to speak. Rosemary had to contend with her. But they got along famously together." [70]

"Sister Paulus was loyal, loving, and supportive of Rosemary," said Mark."[Sister Paulus was] dedicated." [71]

My aunt was an authority figure in Rosie's life, which meant filling in as a father, mother, loving sister, and true friend. I asked Bobby Shriver how he adapted when his aunt and her entourage of nuns turned up at his house for weeks at a time.

"We didn't really adapt," he recalled. "My mom's attitude is, 'Continue doing what you're doing.' The basic ethic is inclusion. Whoever was there was included. No big deal. There were no changes. Same is true with girls in a football game. If the girl cousins walk over, the girls are in the game." [72]

Inclusion—what a concept! Eunice was truly ahead of her time.

As a tribute to his aunt, Bobby Shriver named his second daughter, born in 2009, Rosemary.

When Anthony Shriver had his own family, he continued the family tradition of having Rosemary visit his home for two months each year, a tradition that continued until she passed away. "Rosie had two great skills," Anthony recalled. "She had an avid ability to walk with you multiple blocks [and] enjoy each other's company without having to speak. As a kid, I realized this was calming and sweet. We could move around a neighborhood in stillness with no voice, with unconditional love.

Anthony Shriver and Rosie in Miami

"I also loved swimming with her. She had an enormous ability to tread water in the deep end of the swimming pool. When she was younger, she could jump off of the diving board and have a great smile on her face. At the end of her life, I towed her around the pool and sang to her while she kicked her feet." [73]

Getting Rosemary out of the pool required some effort, because she was tall and heavyset. But Anthony was up to the task, and he relished the opportunity to help.

"It was a great gift," he said. "She gave us the ability and sense of being needed, [as in] when you care for a human being in a complete way. It makes you feel wanted and needed. It makes you feel like you're doing God's work. Rosie gave us that opportunity." [74]

Anthony recalled one time when Rosemary and Sister Paulus visited the Shrivers in Palm Beach, Florida. Anthony and his wife, Alina, took them out for burgers and ice cream. The waitress had brought desserts and Rosie dug into hers. After excusing himself to go to the restroom, Anthony returned to find his Aunt Rosie still eating dessert. "She had her spoon and was finishing off the last touches of *my* ice cream!" he said. "She looked up and smiled at me." [75]

EPILOGUE

In 1985, Sister Paulus and Sister Julaine sat up for several days and nights as they traveled by train from Wisconsin to California. Sister Paulus was then seventy-six years old. By the time I met them at the station in Martinez, California, they were exhausted.

"Why didn't you take the plane?" I asked, incredulous.

"Too expensive," my aunt said.

I strapped my baby in his car seat as the sisters settled into the car. "But Sister, you know Eunice would have paid for it."

"I took a vow of poverty," she said.

"But you're not required to be *miserable*," I said. "I wouldn't sleep sitting up and I'm not in my seventies."

"Next time we'll spring for a sleeping car," she said by way of an accommodation.

There would not be a "next time." I later realized that heroes come in various forms, both ordinary and extraordinary. As a child, I didn't realize I was witnessing heroism in action. My aunt, Sister Paulus, performed heroically on a private stage, while President Kennedy and his family lived and acted heroically in the public arena. My beloved aunt was steadfastly committed to her vows and values; she demonstrated patience and kindness every moment she interacted with Rosie and the other special people at Saint Coletta.

In June 1993, my then eighty-three-year-old aunt accompanied Rosie and another nun to Hyannis Port, as she often did, to visit the Kennedys and the Shrivers. On the third day of her visit, Sister Paulus became ill. She didn't want to go to the hospital. It was not the happiest of occasions; the Kennedy family had gathered for the funeral of Steven Smith, the husband of Rosemary's younger sister Jean. No one was around except a couple of Anthony Shriver's friends.

My aunt was reluctant to bother them and delayed mentioning anything to them until she could no longer stand the pain.

Mrs. Kennedy's personal physician then cared for her. After ten days of thorough tests, he diagnosed a cancerous tumor on her liver.

After the ordeal, my aunt could talk only about the kindness of the Shrivers and the young men who had taken her to the hospital and stayed with her through that first long night.

The Shrivers suggested she stay in Hyannis Port and have their doctors perform the operation. I seconded that plan. But Sister Paulus longed to go home, and she returned to have her surgery performed in Milwaukee. Her health improved for a while and she continued her working "retirement" until later that year when another tumor appeared and she was diagnosed with lung cancer. She opted for no further treatment and moved into a convent for retired sisters in Milwaukee.

In June 1993, Sister Paulus enclosed a note with the Christmas card she sent to all of her friends and relatives. "In June, while vacationing with . . . Sister [. . .] and Rosemary at Hyannis Port, I took very sick. I spent ten days in Cape Cod Hospital; an x-ray showed a malignant tumor on the liver. I returned to Milwaukee and had surgery at St. Joseph's Hospital on July 12. I recuperated at St. Francis Convent, where we have good nurses and friends, until September 1st when I came back to St. Coletta's . . . November 15th a TC scan and check-up showed another tumor. A chest x-ray showed three spots on the lungs. Surgery was cancelled. I'm putting my trust in God and living a day at a time. Please pray for me. I will remember you in my prayers every day. "

She died on March 16, 1996, at the age of eighty-six.

Rosie lived until January 7, 2005, when she, too, was eighty-six years old. For her wake, she lay at her brother Ted's house in the Hyannis Port compound. Because we were largely unknown to the

Kennedy family, we were not invited. However, a Saint Coletta nun sat by Rosie's side. The sister was surprised that Rosie's siblings were asking *her* questions:

"What do you think was wrong with Rosemary?"

"Was she really retarded?"

"No," said the sister. "I believe she was like me. She had problems reading in school, like I did. They called *me* a slow learner."

Even the Kennedy sisters and brother hadn't known the truth about Rosie. The truth hadn't been available when she was first diagnosed, and the Kennedys were so famous, everything had to be kept hidden in case the press or a political opponent got hold of it and decided to use it against them.

Rosemary Kennedy's body is buried in Holyhood Cemetery in Brookline, Massachusetts.

Her obituary didn't list the cause of Rosie's death. I was in my home office when I heard the news, and was struck with sadness first, and then happiness. She had lived a life full of love, both in giving and receiving.

Because I hold a strong belief in the afterlife, I knew Rosie had joined the rest of her family. Shortly after, I dreamt she came to me, looking just as I'd always known her. We smiled, but before either of us could walk closer for a hug, I woke up, excited.

I once asked Sister Paulus why she became a nun. "I felt a calling," she told me. "It's a deep feeling of love when you *know* it's right."

Instinct.

She loved her profession. And she loved Rosie.

And Rosie, thanks ultimately to the Shrivers and the Kennedys, changed the world's perception and treatment of the intellectually challenged forever.

EVENTS AND MEMORIES

While researching this story and contacting friends and family, I received a wealth of photographs of Rosie's life at home and with her extended families. The following pages show these moments of happiness; I am honored to share them.

CHRISTMAS

Rosie unwraps a Christmas gift

Rosie shows the gift she received

Sister Paulus and Rosie pose by poinsettias

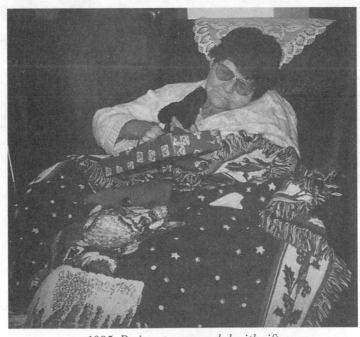

1995, Rosie naps surrounded with gifts

Holiday traditions upheld every year; Rosie and Sister Paulus by the tree

SISTER PAULUS' 50TH JUBILEE

Sister Paulus and Rosie enjoy the Jubilee

Elizabeth, the author, with Rosie ahead of the festivities

Sister Paulus and Rosie

EVERYDAY ROSIE

A moment in the sun during a shopping trip

Rosie in front of Pat's in New York

Rosie at home in her living room

Rosie enjoys sun and waves on a boat ride

Rosie opens gifts

Rosie wears pearls on a very special day

Rosie and Jean

Jean Kennedy Smith, Rosie, and Eunice Kennedy Shriver

Sister Paulus plays with Rosie's dog Lolly

Rosie with Sister Paulus and Father Paul Koehler

Rosie with her friends and family at Saint Coletta

Rosemary Kennedy

September 13, 1918 – January 7, 2005

Stella Koehler/Sister Paulus

December 30, 1910 – March 13, 1996

APPENDIX

JOSEPH P. KENNEDY JR. FOUNDATION

Established in 1946 by Joe and Rose Kennedy in honor of their eldest son, the Foundation first donated money mostly to Catholic groups. Eunice persuaded her father to focus on research and programs addressing mental illness. Her husband, Sargent Shriver, became the director of the Foundation, and together with Eunice, who headed Midwest activities, they forged ahead, consulting experts and conducting their own research.

In 1961, Eunice sought her brother Jack's help and motivated him to create the President's Panel on Mental Retardation. This led to his signing, on October 24, 1963, of the Maternal and Child Health and Mental Retardation Amendment to the Social Security Act, which provided state grants to intellectual disability programs and increased funding for maternity and infant care.

A week later, legislation was approved providing construction funding for institutes, schools, and centers for the prevention, care, and treatment of people with intellectual disabilities. Over the next twenty years, Congress passed 116 acts or amendments focusing on the intellectually disabled and their families.

www.jpkf.org

CAMP SHRIVER

A single camp which was initially located on the grounds of the Shrivers' home in Maryland in 1962 has grown both into Special Olympics and Camp Shriver day camps around the world. "While other summer programs may accept some children with disabilities or offer scholarships to lessen the cost to families, Camp Shriver enrolls an equal number of children with and without disabilities, at no cost to families." [76]

These inclusive camps provide transportation and nourishing meals while instructing campers on sports and team work, and inspiring good social skills.

www.specialolympics.org

SPECIAL OLYMPICS

According to its website, Special Olympics provides "year-round sports training to children and adults with intellectual disabilities, giving them continuing opportunities to develop physical fitness and friendship with their families, other Special Olympics athletes, and the community." [77]

Begun in 1968, Special Olympics now operates world-wide, and serves about 200 million people with intellectual disabilities. Through 33 Olympic-style sports, from badminton to volleyball, judo to roller skating, Special Olympians discover what they *can* do, not what they can't. The games bring volunteers of all ages, nationalities, and communities together. Everyone among various economic groups interact, giving athletes pride, maturity, and social skills.

Athletes from ages 8 and up come from more than 170 countries. In the young athletes' program, children ages 2 ½ to 7 play games that develop motor skills and hand-eye coordination.

Scientific studies have proven that exercise reduces the risk of stroke, heart attacks, depression, and arthritis, improves sleep and mood, and increases energy. In addition to spreading joy and physical fitness to the intellectually challenged, the Kennedy–Shriver message of equality and respect has permeated the world's consciousness and changed how we treat people with disabilities.

www.specialolympics.org

❊❊❊

KENNEDY-DONOVAN CENTER

In January 1961, Joe and Rose Kennedy sent Luella Hennessey Donovan, their private nurse since 1935, to Boston College so she could learn more about mental illnesses. At that time, Jack was coming to the White House as president of the United States.

When Jackie Kennedy asked Luella to move with them into the White House to help with their two young children, Caroline and John Jr., Luella asked the president: "What should I do?"

Jack replied, "There are 96,000 registered nurses in this country. And I think 95,999 would jump at the chance to go to the White House for the winter." [78]

Luella turned down the opportunity to move into the White House and instead pursued her passion—helping people like Rosemary. Rose Kennedy once confided to Luella that she regretted Rosemary's inability to permanently live at home with the family. As a teen, she came home only on weekends. Rose believed special needs children benefited from family life. Early intervention ultimately became a key factor.

When Luella began her studies at Boston College, the institution offered *no* courses that focused on helping people with mental disabilities. Of ninety nurses enrolled in the program, she was the *only one* who indicated any interest in this area of study. The general topic of mental retardation was covered in a single afternoon's trip to a state school.

Instead of giving up, she created her own program. She attended nursing courses in public health and went on to create a survey for the Massachusetts Public Health Department and medical schools throughout the state.

What did she learn? No one knew anything.

Luella received a bachelor's degree in public health and accepted a job in a community where she interacted with families of developmentally delayed children.

Families were in a state of chaos.

Luella said, ". . . The youngsters would be chewing the rug, swinging on the curtains . . . One child bit the tail off a cat when the cat was sleeping!"[79]

Special needs children drained families of their time and energy; families disintegrated. Divorce rates soared; parents were frantic. By the time she reached them, families were so desperate they no longer wanted advice on how to work with their child, or what school to send their challenged child to. They merely wanted to regain a normal family life.

Rose's and Luella's theory of early intervention to save the patient and the family has been proven correct. Luella told Eunice and Ted she wanted to start a program for children starting at the age of 18 months. With no available state or federal monies, the Joseph P. Kennedy Foundation funded it.

In 1969, Luella began the Kennedy-Donovan Center School. Currently, it has twelve locations throughout the state of Massachusetts and assists more than 5,000 individuals and families from over 150 communities. The centers include programs such as early intervention, family and job support, respite care, day school, shared living, and intensive foster care.

Her legacy continues through federal laws, such as The Rehabilitation Act of 1973, which protects people with disabilities from discrimination. The Education for All Handicapped Children Act of 1975 (EHA) allows parents to advocate for their children in administrative hearings, rather than incurring big litigation costs in courts of law. In 1983, the law was amended to include parent training centers at the state level.

Three years later, early intervention programs for infants and preschoolers were added. In 1990, EHA was replaced by the Individuals with Disabilities Education Act, which gives disabled students the right to be educated in their neighborhood public schools instead of separate schools. In addition, each disabled student receives an Individualized Education Program (IEP) to meet his or her specific needs in the least restrictive environment possible. Because of these laws, schools and universities have increased their research and training programs to meet the new criteria.

Through the Kennedy family's encouragement and financial support, and Luella's creative inspiration, determination, and hard work, their legacy continues.

www.kdc.org
Kennedy-Donovan Center, Inc.

BEST BUDDIES INTERNATIONAL

Launched by Anthony Shriver in 1989 while a student at Georgetown University, the first chapter of Best Buddies paired students with and without intellectual and developmental disabilities (IDDs) for friendship and mentoring.

What began as one university chapter has become nearly 1,700 middle school, high school, and college chapters throughout all 50 states and in 50 countries, helping 800,000 people with and without IDDs. Best Buddies' goal is to expand into 100 countries impacting three million people with and without IDDs.

Eight programs make up Best Buddies:

Best Buddies Middle Schools fosters an inclusive school climate at a time of life when social interaction matters the most;

Best Buddies High Schools continues these bonds as students prepare for their futures.

Best Buddies Colleges brings together adults with and without IDDs, preventing isolation.

Best Buddies Promoters empowers youth to advocate for people with and without IDDs.

Best Buddies Citizens creates inclusive friendships and environments in business and civic communities.

e-Buddies presents a safe online forum to develop friendships.

Best Buddies Ambassadors educates and empowers people with IDDs through group training and workshops promoting speaking and leadership skills in their schools, communities, and work environments.

Best Buddies Jobs secures competitive paying work for people with IDDs. Supported by employers, this program aids with hiring and contributes continuing support to employee and employer alike.

Over 25 years, integrated friendships and employment have developed through Best Buddies since its inception, enabling those with IDDs to become happy and productive people.

www.bestbuddies.org

❊❖❊

VSA – EDUCATION
THE JOHN F. KENNEDY CENTER
FOR THE PERFORMING ARTS

In 1974, Rosemary's sister, Jean Kennedy Smith, founded the National Committee-Arts for the Handicapped. In 1985, this organization became Very Special Arts. In 2010, it changed into VSA, which merged with the Kennedy Center's Office on Accessibility to become the Department of VSA and Accessibility at the John F. Kennedy Center for the Performing Arts. Today, seven million intellectually disabled youth and adults participate in art and education, both as creator and as audience member.

Through outreach to schools and communities, VSA assists educators, parents, and art administrators with professional development, holds art contests, creates programs for music, playwriting, and visual art, and stages exhibitions. Research, publications, and webinars are dispensed to educators and administrators.

www.kennedy-center.org/education/vsa

SAINT COLETTA

In 1904, the Sisters of Saint Francis of Assisi opened Saint Coletta in rural Jefferson, Wisconsin, after discovering that state institutions and private homes weren't adequately training intellectually disabled children and adults.

Father George Meyer, the chaplain of Saint Coletta's, said, "It is noble work to train the normally fit and to educate them, but it is a greater work to awaken a dormant and darkened mind to the knowledge of God." [80]

Saint Coletta's, though not begun by the Joseph P. Kennedy Jr. Foundation, has received grants from the Foundation to assist with its programs.

Saint Coletta's school, located across from Highway Y, was down the road from the dormitories. In 1980, St. Coletta began transitioning residents from dorm living to residential group homes.

Today, St. Coletta serves 350 clients through interactive programs of education, recreation, job training and placement, community service, and transportation. Golden Options provides adult day facilities for those who have impairments requiring assistance, or who need personal, social, daily living, and pre-vocational skills.

The work of these sisters "awakens the dormant and darkened minds," [81] both in those with intellectually disabilities *and* those without.

Says Saint Coletta's website: The programs are "inspired by the Franciscan values of compassion, dignity, and respect, and support persons with developmental and other challenges to achieve their highest quality of life, personal growth, and spiritual awareness." [82]

www.stcolettawi.org

President John F. Kennedy's Accomplishments for the Cause

1962: The President's Panel on Mental Retardation proposed one-hundred recommendations for an inclusive federal effort at better care for those with intellectual disabilities.

1963: Maternal and Child Health and Mental Retardation Planning Amendment to the Social Security Act; provided grants for state programs.

Funded construction of facilities related to prevention, care, and treatment of those with intellectual disabilities and to train teachers.

President Kennedy forever changed attitudes regarding those with intellectual disabilities. As he put it, "The mentally ill and the mentally retarded need no longer be alien to our affections or beyond the help of our communities." [83]

TED KENNEDY'S ACCOMPLISHMENTS FOR THE CAUSE

As a United States senator for forty-seven years, Ted Kennedy worked for equality and fairness for everyone. *Some* of the bills he was involved with are as follows:

1964: The Civil Rights Act, which was signed into law by President Lyndon Baines Johnson on July 2, 1964.

1978: Co-sponsored the Civil Rights Commission Act amendments. Protected people from discrimination based on a disability.

1980: Co-sponsored the Civil Rights for Institutionalized Persons Act. Made sure the elderly, the disabled, the mentally ill, and people in prison had all the rights as everyone else in the Constitution. (This helps to prevent and stop abuse and neglect.)

1986: Was an original co-sponsor of the Air Carrier Access Act, which requires the disabled to have equal access to aircrafts, airports, and terminals.

1988: Co-sponsored a bill requiring polling stations to provide physical access to disabled and elderly people voting on election days. They must also make voting aides available.

1990: Helped gain enactment of a law, with Senator Tom Harkin (D-Iowa), of the Americans with Disabilities Act, which broadens the 1964 Civil Rights act to include persons with disabilities. Under ADA, discriminating against people with a physical or mental impairment is against the law.

1998: Co-sponsored the Crime Victims and Disabilities Awareness Act, which studied the issue and created the National Crime Victimization Survey, an annual publication.

2004: Was an original co-sponsor of the Assistive Technology Act, which supported states so they could meet the assistive technology needs of disabled people, such as walkers, wheelchairs, voice-activated computers, etc.

2006: Co-sponsored The Family Opportunity Act expanding Medicaid coverage to children with special needs.

2008: Worked to expand availability of health insurance, which he considered his primary career cause. Although his cancer interrupted his efforts on behalf of the bill, he reappeared, though very ill, to vote and help break a Republican filibuster.

The Kennedy Family Tree

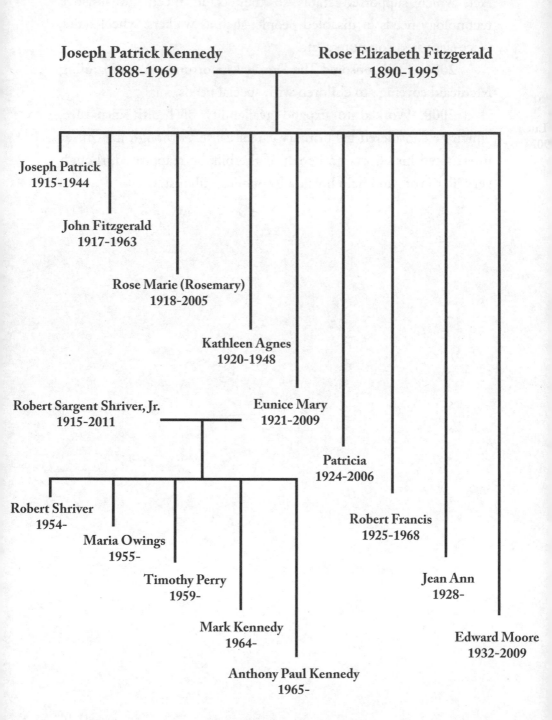

Joseph Patrick Kennedy
1888-1969

Rose Elizabeth Fitzgerald
1890-1995

Joseph Patrick
1915-1944

John Fitzgerald
1917-1963

Rose Marie (Rosemary)
1918-2005

Kathleen Agnes
1920-1948

Robert Sargent Shriver, Jr.
1915-2011

Eunice Mary
1921-2009

Patricia
1924-2006

Robert Shriver
1954-

Maria Owings
1955-

Timothy Perry
1959-

Robert Francis
1925-1968

Mark Kennedy
1964-

Jean Ann
1928-

Anthony Paul Kennedy
1965-

Edward Moore
1932-2009

The Koehler Family Tree

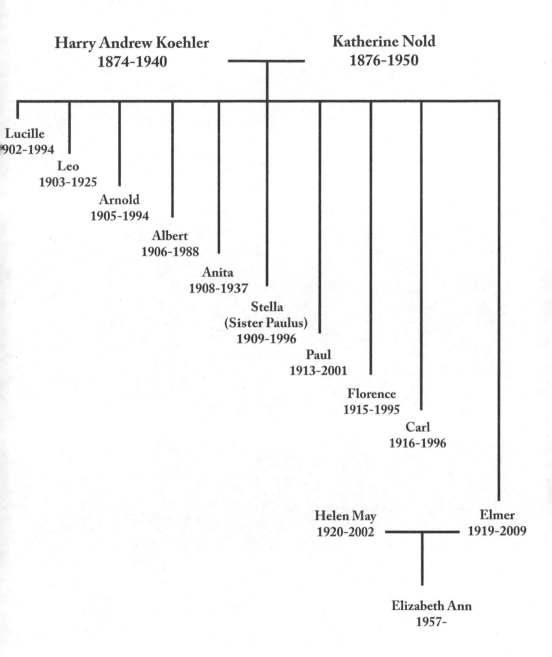

Harry Andrew Koehler
1874-1940

Katherine Nold
1876-1950

Lucille
1902-1994

Leo
1903-1925

Arnold
1905-1994

Albert
1906-1988

Anita
1908-1937

Stella
(Sister Paulus)
1909-1996

Paul
1913-2001

Florence
1915-1995

Carl
1916-1996

Helen May
1920-2002

Elmer
1919-2009

Elizabeth Ann
1957-

END NOTES

For the creation of historic scenes in this book, I'm grateful for the use of the following: conversations and interviews with Sister Paulus Koehler; *Memories* by Sister Paulus Koehler; and *Booklet* by Arnold Koehler.

Best Buddies: *www.bestbuddies.org*

Bobby Shriver: *www.bobbyshriver.com*

Citizen's Energy: *www.citizensenergy.com*

Maria Shriver: *www.mariashriver.com*

Rory Kennedy's Documentary Site: *www.moxiefirecracker.com*

Saint Coletta: *www.stcolettawi.org*

Save the Children: *www.savethechildren.org*

Special Olympics: *www.specialolympics.org*

Very Special Arts: *www.vsarts.org*

Kennedy-Donovan Center: *www.kdc.org*

Abbreviations

JE-H El-Hai, Jack, *The Lobotomist: A Maverick Medical Genius and His Tragic Quest to Rid the World of Mental Illness*. NJ. Wiley. 2005.

PF Fay, Paul B. Jr., *The Pleasure of His Company*. NY. Harper & Row.

1963.

DKG Goodwin, Doris Kearns, *The Fitzgeralds and the Kennedys*. NY. Simon & Schuster, 1987.

EMK Kennedy, Edward M., *True Compass: A Memoir*. NY. Grand Central Publishing. 2009.

RK Kennedy, Rose Fitzgerald, *Times to Remember*. NY. Doubleday. 1974.

LL Leamer, Laurence, *The Kennedy Women: The Saga of an American Family*. NY. Villard. 1994.

JP Pressman, Jack, *The Last Resort: Psychosurgery and the Limits of Medicine*, UK.

ES Shorter, Edward, *The Kennedy Family and the Story of Mental Retardation*. PA. Temple University Press. 2000.

AS Smith, Amanda, *Hostage To Fortune: The Letters of Joseph P. Kennedy*. NY. Putnam. 2001

ESV Valenstein, Elliot S., *Great and Desperate Cures: The Rise and Decline of Psychosurgery and Other Radical Treatments for Mental Illness*. 2010

1) "She was slow in everything . . ." RK, p. 141
2) ". . . My first reaction was" and "How Rosemary Brought Strength to Us," Family Weekly August 3, 1975
3) *"It was nerve wracking . . ." ibid.*
4) "I recalled the gentle . . ." EMK, p. 399
5) "It was a nice . . ." RK, p. 65
6) "Rose, this is a helluva . . ." RK, p. 204
7) Do you know . . .": PF, p. 124
8) "sober eighteenth-century. . ." Vogue, August 3, 1938

9) "The American Ambassador . . ." *ibid.*

10) "Mrs. Kennedy wore . . ." New York Times, May 1938

11) "Miss Rosemary Kennedy . . ."The Evening Standard, May 12, 1938

12) "glittering with diamonds . . ." New York Times, May 1938

13) "Well Daddy . . ." AS, p. 412

14) "Why don't other . . ." and "Rosemary Brought Us Strength," Catholic Digest, March 1976

15) "In one traumatic . . . *The Kennedys: An American Drama* Collier, Peter & Horowitz, David, Simon & Schuster, Inc., 1984

16) "Oh, Mother, no . . ." LL, p. 319

17) "I, Stella Koehler . . ." Archives of the Sisters of St. Francis of Asissi.

18) The Prayer of St. Francis

19) "agitated depression" JE-H, p. 174

20) "one bed for ..." ESV, p. 61

21) "I have seen coleslaw . . ." and "Bedlam," Life, May 6, 1946

22) "dribbling blood . . ." JE-H, p. 74

23) "Freeman thrived on . . ." JP

24) "would stand by . . ." ESV, p. 160, James Watts, "Psychosurgery: The Story of the 20 Year Follow-up of the Freeman and Watts Lobotomy Series," unpublished speech presented Nov. 5, 1974

25) "No worse . . . Wizardry of" p. 69, Dully, Howard, *My Lobotomy*, Crown, NY, 2007

26) "blunt spatula—much . . ." ESV, p. 149

27) "surgery of the soul" JE-H p. 123, New York Times, "Surgery Used on the Soul-Sick," June 6, 1937

28) "The first ice pick . . ." American Experience, "The Lobotomist," PBS, Alfred P. Sloan Foundation, 2008

29) "lobotomobile" Dully, Howard, and Fleming, Charles, *My Lobotomy*, Crown, NY, p. 71

30) "We believe he . . ." Anthony Shriver, personal interview, Dec. 1, 2010

31) "When you do . . ." Dr. Steven Holtz, personal interview, Sept. 17, 2012

32) *Ibid.*

33) "ornately carved dark . . ." Fortune, April 1935, "The Nervous Breakdown, Sanitariums."

34) "Each patient has . . ." *ibid.*

35) "practical psychotherapy," Fortune, April 1935, "The Nervous Breakdown, Sanitariums."

36) "A douche of hot . . ." Stedman, Thomas Lathrop, *A Practical Dictionary*, 1920

37) "warm shallow baths . . ." *www.healthline.com*

38) Dr. C.J. Slocum, undated letter

39) Email to Robert Murphy, May 28, 2011, from an unnamed resident of the Sargent Estate

40) "If a mosquito . . ." RK, p. 187

41) "It was involuntary . . ." John F. Kennedy and PT 109, *www.jfklibrary.org*

42) "Don't let it be . . ." Lerner, Alan Jay, "Camelot," Vocal Selection, January 1, 1960

43) "Joey, we must . . ." LL, p. 592

44) "frustrating and dismal" Eunice Kennedy speech, President's Committee on the Employment of the Handicapped, 1963, Washington Post, May 10, 1963

45) "have received virtually . . ." *ibid.*

46) "You should put . . ." LL, p. 75

47) "I lost her." Koehler, Sister Paulus letter, Sept. 14, 1975

48) "Traveling alone with . . ." Koehler, Sister Paulus, *Memories*, undated

49) "She was just . . ." Anthony Shriver, personal interview, Dec. 1, 2010

50) "One assumes she . . ." Dr. Steven Holtz, personal interview, Sept. 17, 2012

51) "An individual who . . ." Dr. Steven Holtz, personal interview, Sept. 16, 2104

52) *Ibid.*

53) "What an enormous . . ." Bobby Shriver, personal interview, Aug. 3, 2011

54) "She never complained . . ." and "The Kennedy Case," Rita Dallas, McCall's, June 1973

55) "I remember Grandma . . ." Bobby Shriver, personal interview, Aug. 3, 2011

56) "a certain form . . ." RK, p. 263

57) "I was seven . . ." Bobby Shriver, personal interview, Aug. 3, 2011

58) "Special people were . . ." *ibid*

59) "When I'd come . . ." ES, p. 114

60) "depicting retarded children . . ." ES p. 131

61) "Nobody is turned . . ." *www.specialolympics.com*

62) "You know, Eunice" *ibid*

63) "My mother was . . ." Anthony Shriver, personal interview, Dec.1, 2010

64) We judge a book . . ." Timothy Shriver, "Inside Politics," Judy Woodruff, *www.cnn.com*, Jan. 14, 2005

65) "I remember Rosemary . . ." Bobby Shriver, personal interview, Aug. 3, 2011

66) "She'd tell . . ." Anthony Shriver, personal interview, Dec. 1, 2010

67) *Ibid.*

68) "She treated Rosemary . . ." Mark Shriver, personal interview, June 27, 2013

69) "Sister Paulus was . . ." *ibid.*

70) "I'd see how Rosie . . ." Bobby Shriver, personal interview, Aug. 3, 2011

71) "Sister Paulus was . . ." Mark Shriver, personal interview, June 27, 2013

72) "We didn't really . . ." Bobby Shriver, personal interview, Aug. 3, 2011

73) Rosie had two . . ." Anthony Shriver, personal interview, Dec. 1, 2010

74) "It was a great gift . . ." *ibid.*

75) "She had her spoon . . ." *ibid.*

76) *www.specialolympics.org*

77) *Ibid.*

78) Luella Hennessey-Donovan Oral History Interview, John F. Kennedy Oral History Collection, John F. Kennedy Presidential Library, Sept. 25, 1991

79) *Ibid.*

80) Hegeman, Sister Mary Theodore, OSF, "History of St. Coletta," Jefferson, Wisconsin, 1904-1994

81) *Ibid.*

82) *www.st.colettawi.org*

83) *www.jfklibrary.org*

BIBLIOGRAPHY

Cameron, Gail, *Rose: A Biography of Rose Fitzgerald Kennedy*. NY. Putnam. 1971.

Dully, Howard and Fleming, Charles, *My Lobotomy*. NY. Three Rivers Press. 2007.

El-Hai, Jack, *The Lobotomist: A Maverick Medical Genius and His Tragic Quest to Rid the World of Mental Illness*. NJ. Wiley. 2005.

Fay, Paul B. Jr., *The Pleasure of His Company*. NY. Harper & Row. 1963.

Goodwin, Doris Kearns, *The Fitzgeralds and the Kennedys*. NY. Simon & Schuster, 1987.

Haskins, James, *A New Kind of Joy: The Story of the Special Olympics*. NY. Doubleday. 1976.

John F. Kennedy Library Foundation, *Rose Kennedy's Family Album*. NY. Grand Central Publishing. 2013.

Kennedy, Edward M., *True Compass: A Memoir*. NY. Grand Central Publishing. 2009.

Kennedy, Jacqueline, *Jacqueline Kennedy: Historic Conversations on Life with John F. Kennedy*. NY. Hyperion. 2011.

Kennedy, Rose Fitzgerald, *Times to Remember*. NY. Doubleday. 1974.

Leamer, Laurence, *The Kennedy Women: The Saga of an American Family*. NY. Villard. 1994.

Leamer, Laurence, *The Sons of Camelot: The Fate of An American Dynasty*. NY. HarperCollins. 2004.

Matthews, Chris, *Jack Kennedy, Elusive Hero*. NY. Simon & Schuster. 2011.

Pressman, Jack, *The Last Resort: Psychosurgery and the Limits of Medicine*, UK. Cambridge University Press, 1998.

Price, Holly and Stegemeyer, Ann, *Who's Who in Fashion*. NY. Fairchild. 2009.

Shorter, Edward, *The Kennedy Family and the Story of Mental Retardation*. PA. Temple University Press. 2000.

Smith, Amanda, *Hostage To Fortune: The Letters of Joseph P. Kennedy*. NY. Putnam. 2001.

Swift, Will, *The Kennedys: Amidst The Gathering Storm: A Thousand Days in London, 1938-1940*. HarperCollins. 2008

Valenstein, Elliot S., *Great and Desperate Cures: The Rise and Decline of Psychosurgery and Other Radical Treatments for Mental Illness*. 2010.

PHOTO CREDITS

ROSEMARY'S CHILDHOOD

All photos in this chapter are presented courtesy of John F. Kennedy Library

p. 3 Three happy Kennedy children: Rosie, Jack, and Joe
p. 4 Five gorgeous Kennedy kids: Rosie, Jack, Joe, Kathleen, and Eunice
p. 5 Rosie enjoys a three-wheeler by the sea
p. 7 Rosie's First Communion, 1926
p. 9 Rosie as a freckle-faced fifteen year old

MY AUNT STELLA

All photos in this chapter are courtesy of Elizabeth Koehler-Pentacoff's Private Collection

p. 13 Saint Bruno's Church
p. 14 Stella (right) at her First Communion
p. 17 Elmer Koehler and the author as a child on the Homestead Farm
p. 19 Holy Hill
p. 21 The Koehler family together, 1923

FIRST HOMES

p. 24 The Kennedys' house Courtesy of National Park Service, John Fitzgerald Kennedy National Historic Site, Matt Teuten, Photographer
p. 26 Koehler farmhouse Elizabeth Koehler-Pentacoff Private Collection
p. 27 Rosemary's childhood bedroom Courtesy of National park Service, John Fitzgerald Kennedy National Historic Site, Robert Perron, Photographer
p. 29 The Koehler family farmstead Elizabeth Koehler-Pentacoff
p. 30 & p. 31 The Author's mother Elizabeth Koehler-Pentacoff

ENGLAND

p. 39: Kathleen, Rose and Rosemary Courtesy of Corbis Images
p. 41 Rosemary dances with family friend, Edward Moore Courtesy Peter Hunter/ Otto Salomen.

Rosemary and Stella in Their Twenties

Stella becomes Sister Paulus

Rosemary's Surgery

Aunt Zora

Uncle Nick

Rosie at Saint Coletta

All photos in this chapter are courtesy of Elizabeth Koehler-Pentacoff's Private Collection

TRAGEDY

MY MISDIAGNOSIS

All photos in this chapter are courtesy of Elizabeth Koehler-Pentacoff's Private Collection

EUNICE

All photos in this chapter are courtesy of Elizabeth Koehler-Pentacoff's Private Collection

SEX ED AND SILENCE

THE KOEHLER BRAND OF CLAUSTROPHOBIC CATHOLICISM

ROSIE'S THREE FAMILIES

All photos in this chapter are courtesy of Elizabeth Koehler-Pentacoff's Private Collection

STANDING OUT

All photos in this chapter are courtesy of Elizabeth Koehler-Pentacoff's Private Collection

SPECIAL OLYMPICS

The following images are courtesy of Elizabeth Koehler-Pentacoff's Private Collection

EVENTS AND MEMORIES

All photos in this chapter are courtesy of Elizabeth Koehler-Pentacoff's Private Collection

ABOUT THE AUTHOR

About the Author

Elizabeth Koehler-Pentacoff is the author of nine books, including a Writer's Digest Selection for *The ABCs of Writing for Children*. *The Missing Kennedy* is her first memoir.

A former *Byline Magazine* "Writing for Children" columnist, Liz wrote frequent humor pieces for the *San Francisco Examiner* as well as hundreds of articles and essays for newspapers and magazines such as *Parents Magazine, Writer's Digest,* and *Parenting.*

With degrees in Liberal Studies and Theater Arts/Children's Theater and two teaching credentials, she's directed plays and taught elementary, middle school students, and teachers. A speaker for international and state conferences, she presents assemblies and workshops for schools and libraries.

Born in rural Wisconsin, Liz moved to California for all her college and post-graduate education (California State University, Fresno), and has lived most of her adult life in the San Francisco area. She is married and has one grown child.

Information on upcoming books and tour dates can be found at her website: *www.lizbooks.com.*

For writing advice, ideas, and anecdotes, visit her blog: *www.lizbooks.com/blog.*